Food Poisoning and Foodborne Diseases
(Diseases and People)

Latta, Sara L.
AR B.L.: 9.1
Points: 3.0                    UG

# FOOD POISONING AND FOODBORNE DISEASES

*Other titles in* Diseases and People

—Diseases and People—

# FOOD POISONING AND FOODBORNE DISEASES

Sara L. Latta

**Enslow Publishers, Inc.**

| 40 Industrial Road | PO Box 38 |
| Box 398 | Aldershot |
| Berkeley Heights, NJ 07922 | Hants GU12 6BP |
| USA | UK |

http://www.enslow.com

**Library of Congress Cataloging-in-Publication Data**

Latta, Sara L.
    Food poisoning and foodborne diseases / Sara L. Latta.
        p. cm. (Diseases and people)
    Includes bibliographical references and index.
    Summary: Examines food poisoning and foodborne diseases, discussing their history,
symptoms, effects, diagnosis, treatment, and prevention.
    ISBN 0-7660-1183-6
    1. Food poisoning—Juvenile literature. 2. Foodborne diseases —Juvenile literature.
[1. Food poisoning. 2. Foodborne diseases.] I. Title. II. Series.
RA601.5.L38  1999
615.9'54—dc21                         98-36134
                                        CIP
                                        AC

Printed in the United States of America

10 9 8 7 6 5 4 3 2 1

**To Our Readers:**
All Internet addresses in this book were active and appropriate when we went to press. Any
comments or suggestions can be sent by e-mail to Comments@enslow.com or to the address
on the back cover.

**Illustration Credits:** © Corel Corporation, pp. 12, 25, 33, 41, 78, 83, 97; Image
by David E. Graham, Cornell University, 1995, p. 42; Iowa State University, p. 93;
© Tony M. Liss, 1998, pp. 45, 58, 69, 72, 75; National Library of Medicine, p. 20;
Partnership for Food Safety Education, p. 62.

**Cover Illustration:** © Corel Corporation.

# Contents

# FOOD POISONING AND FOODBORNE DISEASES

**What are food poisoning and foodborne diseases?** Broadly speaking, a foodborne disease is any illness caused by eating food contaminated with disease-causing microbes (viruses, bacteria, or parasites), toxins, or chemicals. The term *food poisoning* is usually reserved for illness caused by toxins or chemicals. This book focuses on foodborne diseases or food poisoning caused by viruses, parasites, and bacteria or their toxins.

**Who gets foodborne diseases?** Anyone can get a foodborne disease. An estimated 6.5 to 33 million Americans become ill after eating food contaminated with disease-causing microbes each year. Some people, including those with weakened immune systems, are more susceptible to the illness.

**What are the symptoms?** Because foodborne diseases are caused by a variety of bacteria, viruses, and parasites, the symptoms can vary. Common symptoms are nausea, vomiting, abdominal cramps, and diarrhea.

**How are foodborne diseases treated?** In most instances, foodborne diseases are best treated with bed rest and replacement of lost fluids. More serious cases may require hospitalization.

**How can foodborne diseases be prevented?** It is impossible to keep food *completely* free of disease-causing microbes, but there are some things you can do to lessen the risk of foodborne disease. Thoroughly cook all meat, poultry, and fish products. Keep hot foods hot and cold foods cold. Do not spread bacteria from raw meat and poultry to other food or surfaces. Wash your hands with warm, soapy water before preparing food, after handling fresh meat, poultry, or fish, and after using the bathroom.

# Foodborne Disease Today

It was a typically busy Saturday for the Kiner family. Suzanne Kiner asked her husband to cook dinner for their two youngest daughters while she took their oldest daughter, an oboist, to a rehearsal. Rex Kiner offered to pick up some burgers at the nearby Jack in the Box restaurant instead. Brianne Kiner, a bright, bouncy nine-year-old girl with long brown hair, ordered a cheeseburger—the second fast-food burger she had ever eaten. Over the next couple of days, Brianne and her sister Karin, who also ate a Jack in the Box burger, developed flulike symptoms and diarrhea. Karin recovered, but Brianne kept getting sicker. Her diarrhea turned bloody, and she began having severe abdominal cramps. She was admitted to the hospital, and soon fell into a coma that lasted almost six weeks.

Brianne is among the nearly five hundred people known to have become ill during a 1992–1993 outbreak of foodborne illness in the western United Sates. Most of the cases were traced to undercooked hamburgers served by the Jack in the Box restaurant chain. Four people died as a result of their illness.[1]

The hamburgers were tainted with *Escherichia coli* O157:H7, an especially nasty strain of bacteria found in the intestines of warm-blooded animals. These bacteria, called *E. coli* O157:H7 for short, produce a potent toxin that can cause severe damage to the intestine, kidneys, and other vital organs. Brianne became so ill that the doctors thought the end was near. Hoping to discover the cause of her illness, they asked her mother if they could perform an autopsy. Suzanne Kiner responded with typical black humor: "Can she die first?"[2]

Brianne did not die. After 189 days in the hospital, she was well enough to go home. Now fifteen years old, Brianne is in many ways a typical teenager. But her pancreas, an organ that produces the body's insulin, was so severely damaged that she is now diabetic. Her entire large intestine had to be removed, and her immune system does not work as well as it once did. "Her doctors say she can't take another intestinal hit," said Brianne's mother[3]—meaning that she might not survive another attack of foodborne illness.

## Millions Suffer from Foodborne Disease

Although Brianne's illness was unusually severe, an estimated 6.5 to 33 million Americans become ill each year after eating food tainted with disease-causing microbes or their products. Disease detectives are not always able to determine the cause of foodborne disease. For those cases in which researchers do identify the agent, 90 percent are caused by bacteria or the toxins they produce.[4]

Microbes are just about everywhere. They live in the guts of animals, under the Antarctic ice, and in your kitchen sink. The vast majority of microbes are not only harmless, they are downright helpful. We have billions of bacteria—including varieties of *E. coli*—that live in our own intestines. They help us digest and absorb nutrients from our food, and they crowd out microbes that could make us ill.

There are, however, a handful of microbes called pathogens that can make us very sick. They can be bacteria, viruses, fungi, or protozoa (a kind of one-celled parasite). This book will focus on some of the most important pathogens that hitch a ride into our bodies through the food we eat.

For many people, "food poisoning" means nausea, vomiting, abdominal cramps, and diarrhea. Most cases are not serious and clear up within a day or two without medical care. But disease-causing microbes are a motley crew. Depending on the type and quantity of microbe consumed, and the medical condition of the patient, foodborne diseases can be life-threatening. The onset of disease can be sudden, within a few hours after eating contaminated food, or gradual, even up to a month. Some foodborne diseases can have long-lasting effects.

In most cases, treating foodborne disease simply means bed rest and replacing fluids that are lost through vomiting and diarrhea. Antibiotics are not always helpful, and in some cases may kill off some of the "good" intestinal bacteria that inhibit the growth of pathogens.

The foods most likely to cause human illness are animal products such as red meat, poultry, eggs, seafood, and dairy products, although contaminated fruits and vegetables are becoming a serious problem as well. Tiny amounts of animal feces can transfer microbes that live harmlessly in the intestines of animals, such as the one that nearly killed Brianne, onto the food we eat. Some disease-causing microbes

Some microbes that can cause foodborne diseases live in the intestinal tract of animals, including beef cattle.

live in the water and are carried to our tables in undercooked seafood. Parasites can live in the tissues of infected animals. Other microbes lie dormant in the soil and grow only under certain conditions such as improperly canned food. Some people are infected with disease-causing microbes without being sick themselves. These people, called carriers, can spread diseases if they do not practice good hygiene when preparing food for others.

Foodborne diseases cause untold human misery, in developing and industrialized countries alike. The World Health Organization (WHO) estimates that about 70 percent of the 1.5 billion yearly cases of diarrhea in children under the age of five are caused by microbes; 3 million of these children will die from their disease.[5] Foodborne diseases may cause as many as nine thousand deaths each year in the United States alone.[6] The United States Department of Agriculture (USDA) estimates that just six types of foodborne pathogens account for 2.9 to 6.7 billion dollars in medical costs and loss of productivity every year.[7]

Practicing good hygiene—especially washing your hands with warm, soapy water after using the rest room—is one of the most important things you can do to prevent the spread of foodborne illness. It is also a good idea to assume that all food is contaminated with pathogens, and to take steps to kill the microbes or prevent them from growing. The burden of responsibility for safe food also rests on those who produce, process, and sell the food. Various government agencies are responsible for ensuring that certain safety standards are met,

# The Naming of Microbes

Just as animals and plants have scientific titles, so do microbes. Under the scientific naming system developed by the eighteenth-century Swedish naturalist Carolus Linnaeus, for example, humans belong to the genus called *Homo*, and the species known as *sapiens*. *Escherichia coli* O157:H7 belongs to the genus *Escherichia* (named after its discoverer, Theodor Escherich) and to the species *coli* (meaning that it lives in the intestine, or colon). Within a species, there are often different but closely related "strains." The letters and numbers following the species name refer to proteins on the surface of the bacteria that are specific to this particular strain. The names of microbes can get awfully long, so the genus name is often abbreviated to an initial. For example, *Escherichia coli* O157:H7 is usually called *E. coli* O157:H7.

Viruses also have two-part scientific names, but in many cases they are not widely used. The hepatitis A virus is so named because it is one of a group of viruses that cause liver disease; the Norwalk virus is named for the Ohio town where it was first discovered.

and for tracking foodborne disease outbreaks when they do occur.

Researchers are focusing on ways to avoid foodborne diseases. Scientists are developing new methods for detecting even tiny amounts of foodborne microbes, and for inhibiting the growth of pathogens on food or killing them outright. New vaccines may protect people and, in some cases, pathogen-carrying animals from infection.

# 2

# The History of
# Foodborne Disease

**N**o one really knows when humans began to make the connection between food and illness, but it might have gone something like this:

"There you are behind that bush again, George. What on earth are you doing?"

"I've got the 'trots,' Gertrude. I think I'm going to die."

"You and nearly every other man in the clan. The only man who is not sick is Bernie, and, of course, we women and children are fine."

"Why us, Gertrude?"

"I have a theory. You refused to share your leftover mastodon meat with the women and children, so we were forced to eat leaves and berries. Bernie did not eat any meat either. He said it smelled bad. I *told* you to store it in the snowbank instead of leaving it on the floor of the cave, but no, you were too tired. I think that rotten meat made you sick."

The connection between foodborne illness and food safety might not have been discovered in *exactly* that manner, but scholars do know that humans learned fairly early on to preserve their food. They cooked, smoked, dried, fermented, and salted it—all methods that prevent or slow the growth of bacteria. Of course, they had no idea that tiny living creatures could make them sick.

The Roman philosopher Lucretius, who lived during the first century B.C., did suggest that disease might be caused by invisible living creatures, but few people accepted his theory. Even after the Dutch lens-maker Antonie van Leeuwenhoek described the remarkable living creatures he found under his microscope in 1676, the idea that these microbes might make people sick seemed ridiculous. You might as well entertain the notion that a mouse could kill an elephant.

Still, people were aware that certain foods that were usually wholesome could occasionally make them sick. By the nineteenth century, many thought that chemical poisons produced in spoiled food caused illness such as nausea and diarrhea. They called these poisons "ptomaines" (from the Greek word *ptoma*, meaning "corpse").

There were problems with the ptomaine theory, though. On the one hand, spoiled food—food that is no longer fit to eat because bacteria or molds have begun to grow in or on it— did not always cause illness. On the other hand, a glass of fresh, sweet-smelling milk might cause diarrhea, fever, or even death. In 1857, an Englishman named William Taylor showed that milk could transmit typhoid fever. No one really knew why, but by this time it was clear that milk and other foods produced or stored under unsanitary conditions often caused disease. We now know that the microbes, which cause food to spoil, do not necessarily make you sick. In fact, the bacteria or molds responsible for spoiling food may prevent the growth of harmful microbes.

## The Birth of Bacteriology

The work of the French chemist Louis Pasteur, and his German rival Robert Koch, marked the birth of a new science called bacteriology, the study of microbes. From 1863 to 1876, Pasteur showed that microbes could spoil wine and beer. He recommended that wine and beer be heated during production—a process we now call pasteurization—to prevent them from going sour. By 1880, Germany began to pasteurize milk as well. People are often slow to accept new food-processing technologies, however, and pasteurization was slow to catch on in the rest of the world. Some feared that the process would make milk less nutritious or lead to the formation of harmful by-products. Others were afraid that farmers, knowing their milk would later be pasteurized, might be less careful about sanitation. The public eventually overcame its fears of the new technology, and by 1939, most milk sold in the United States was pasteurized.[1]

Pasteur was quick to recognize that his work might have broader significance. "When we see beer and wine undergoing profound changes because these liquids have furnished a refuge for microscopic organisms," Pasteur wrote, "how can we avoid the thought that phenomena of the same order can and must be found sometimes in the case of men and animals."[2]

Pasteur's theories were truly revolutionary, but Robert Koch was responsible for some of the most important techniques in the new science of bacteriology. Koch developed methods for growing pure strains of bacteria in the laboratory and established strict criteria for showing that a specific microbe caused a specific disease. By the late 1880s, scientists using Koch's methods had identified the bacteria that cause a number of diseases, including some foodborne illnesses.

In 1888, there was an outbreak of meat poisoning in Frankenhausen, Germany. A cow with diarrhea had been slaughtered for meat. Fifty-nine people became ill; one man died. The meat was probably contaminated with the animal's feces, which were almost certainly loaded with the microbes that caused the diarrhea. A German scientist, A. Gärtner, isolated a type of bacterium that he named *Bacillus enteritidis*, from the meat and from the man who died. Gärtner's bacterium would later be named *Salmonella enteritidis*. This bacterium is part of a large family of microbes that includes *Salmonella typhi*, the cause of typhoid fever. Today, *S. enteritidis* and other members from this family are significant causes of foodborne illness.

In 1895, twenty-four members of a music club took part in a wake in Belgium. As at many wakes, there was food—in this case, an uncooked, salted ham. One or two days later,

Foodborne diseases were all too common in the eighteenth century. This cookbook photo shows an eighteenth-century kitchen, well-equipped for its time.

twenty-three of the twenty-four club members became wretchedly ill. Their muscles became weak, and breathing was difficult. They had botulism, an often fatal disease related to eating sausage or other preserved or canned foods (the Latin word *botulus* means "sausage"). Three of the musicians died within a week, and at least ten came close to dying. Emile van Ermengem, a professor at the University of Ghent in Belgium, investigated the outbreak. He was determined to find the true cause of botulism.

Van Ermengem isolated a type of bacterium that he named *Bacillus botulinus* (now called *Clostridium botulinum*), both from the ham and from one of the victims' internal organs.[3] Later, van Ermengem showed that the bacteria could grow and multiply only in oxygen-free containers and that botulism itself is actually caused by a powerful poison, or toxin, produced by the microbe. Furthermore, he showed that heat would destroy the toxin and that high levels of salt content would prevent *C. botulinum* from producing the toxin. Based on his findings, van Ermengem cautioned the public that preserved food should always be properly cooked and thrown out altogether if it smells bad.

Since the late nineteenth century, researchers had suspected—but not proven—that a bacterium called *Staphylococcus aureus* could cause foodborne illness. Staph poisoning, as it is often called, is no fun, but it does not last long and is usually not very serious. This may be why Dr. M. A. Barber was willing to experiment on himself with the bacterium. In 1914, Barber had made several visits to a farm in the Philippines,

21

and on three occasions he had become ill. Barber suspected the cream from the farm's two cows, one of which had an udder infection. Barber thought that the microbe responsible for the cow's udder infection might also be the cause of his own illness.

Barber took home two bottles of cream. He left them out on the counter for five hours so that any microbes present in the milk would have a chance to grow. Barber then drank some of the cream. Two hours later, he began vomiting and had diarrhea—the same symptoms he had had on the farm. Even though he was feeling very sick, he managed to isolate a single type of bacterium from the milk, a microbe that grew in yellow clumps, or colonies. Following Koch's guidelines for identifying the bacterial culprit, Barber put some of the yellow microbes into a container of germ-free milk. After a period of time, he convinced two volunteers to drink this milk along with him. Sure enough, they all became ill within two hours.

It was not until 1930 that a University of Chicago researcher, Gail M. Dack, proved—also using human volunteers—that *S. aureus* makes a toxin. He showed that eating the toxin, and not the microbe itself, is the cause of staphylococcal food poisoning. Although staph food poisoning continues to be a significant problem, the number of outbreaks has declined in recent years.[4]

By 1939, food microbiologists knew the basic principles of food safety. They knew that food should be kept as clean as possible, because even a tiny bit of feces or dirt could contain large numbers of disease-causing microbes. They learned to kill any remaining microbes with heat if possible, and prevent the rest from growing in the food. The canning industry learned effective ways of protecting against botulism. After a number of outbreaks of such milkborne diseases as brucellosis, tuberculosis, diphtheria, and typhoid fever, public health officials established requirements concerning animal health, sanitation, pasteurization, and refrigeration. Nevertheless, food microbiologists continued to isolate other disease-causing foodborne organisms—bacteria, viruses, and microscopic one-celled organisms called protozoa.

## The Changing Face of Foodborne Illness

By the 1960s, medical science had made tremendous progress toward preventing and treating infectious diseases, including foodborne diseases. In 1967, United States surgeon general William H. Stewart was so optimistic that he said it was time to close the book on infectious disease.[5] It has since become clear that Stewart and others who shared his optimism were terribly wrong. More people are getting sick from foodborne and other infectious diseases than ever before. New disease-causing microbes are making their way into our food supply, and old threats such as *Salmonella enteritidis* have found new routes to our stomachs and intestines. These "emerging foodborne diseases" have become a major public health threat.

Why are we suddenly threatened with new foodborne diseases? Scientists at the Centers for Disease Control and Prevention (CDC) have identified several reasons.[6] The first has to do with who we are. A growing number of people in the United States have weak immune systems because they are infected with HIV (human immunodeficiency virus) or because they are old or have some chronic disease. As you will read in Chapter 3, a healthy immune system is an important defense against any microbial infection, including those we might get from contaminated food.

Our eating habits have changed as well. We eat more fresh fruits and vegetables year-round than ever before. These foods are good for the heart, but they also have the potential for carrying more disease-causing microbes.[7] Organically grown produce may be fertilized with composted animal manure that still harbors disease-causing organisms. Even conventionally grown produce may become accidentally contaminated with animal feces.

We eat out more. Restaurants sometimes use techniques such as maintaining prepared foods at temperatures that allow low numbers of microbes to grow and multiply.

We travel more, too. People who travel abroad sometimes bring home unwanted "souvenirs" that they can pass on to others. In California, brucellosis (a disease that affects cows) used to be most common among people who worked with animals for a living. Now, brucellosis in California most commonly affects Hispanics who consume raw milk or cheese made with raw milk while abroad.[8]

In the last fifty years, we have drastically changed the ways in which we produce, process, and distribute our food. In 1945, for example, a typical henhouse contained five hundred birds. If a few birds became infected with *Salmonella*, it was fairly easy for the farmer to prevent the spread of disease.

Even a fine restaurant can make mistakes. Do not be shy about sending food back to the chef if your meal appears to be improperly cooked.

By 1995, one hundred thousand hens could live in one house, with several houses connected by common machinery. It became much more difficult for the farmer to limit the spread of the bacteria.[9]

Giant processing plants, once unheard of, sometimes lead to large outbreaks of foodborne illness. In 1985, one of the largest dairy processing plants in the Midwest was responsible for nearly two hundred thousand cases of salmonellosis. Each day, the plant processed about 1.5 million pounds of raw milk from southern Wisconsin and northern Illinois dairies and delivered most of it to one large chain of grocery stores. Investigators believe that a small amount of contaminated raw milk somehow made its way into huge vats of already pasteurized milk.[10] What might have been a limited outbreak of salmonellosis became widespread. This outbreak was especially disturbing because the microbe responsible for all those illnesses, *Salmonella typhimurium*, was resistant to antimicrobial drugs.

Like all other living things, bacteria change and evolve over time—only faster. *Salmonella enteritidis* adapted to be able to live in the gastrointestinal tract of animals and birds. In the past, if the bacteria in hens' intestines ever entered their eggs, it was from the outside in, through cracks in the shell. But in recent decades, *S. enteritidis* has gained the ability to also infect the ovaries, or female reproductive organs, of even healthy-looking chickens. *S. enteritidis* in the hens' ovaries could now pass directly to their eggs, before the shells are even formed. The once-common practice of eating foods containing raw or lightly cooked eggs is no longer safe, but old habits die hard. Grade A shell eggs continue to be associated with most *S. enteritidis* outbreaks.

Today, it is common in the livestock industry to feed animals low levels of antibiotics. This practice helps the animals grow faster, but unfortunately it has also encouraged the development of antibiotic-resistant bacteria.[11] The practice may also have encouraged the development of a new, sometimes deadly strain of *Escherichia coli* O157:H7. Most strains of *E. coli* are harmless; in fact, these are some of the "good guys"— called normal flora—that live in your gut.

But this new *E. coli* had picked up a toxin from another type of bacterium—*Shigella*—that could cause bloody diarrhea

# John Snow and the Broad Street Pump

Throughout history, cholera has been one of the most devastating and feared diseases; it causes severe diarrhea, dehydration (serious water loss), fever, and often death. We now know that it is caused by water or food contaminated with human feces or sewage containing the bacteria *Vibrio cholerae*.

When cholera hit the city of London in 1848, officials blamed "bad air" from the poorer sections of town. Never mind the fact that the city's chief water supply, the Thames River, was badly polluted with raw sewage.

John Snow, a medical doctor in London, noticed that there was a cluster of cholera cases in one neighborhood. Those who drew their water from a well on Broad Street, he found, were nine times more likely to die than people in the same neighborhood who used water from another well.

Snow persuaded city officials to remove the handle from the Broad Street pump. Now the residents were forced to get their water from another pump, and the cholera cases dropped immediately. Snow later showed that the water from the Broad Street pump was supplied by a company that drew from an especially polluted part of the Thames.

Snow did not show that microbes caused cholera, but his detective work has become a classic of epidemiology— the study of the spread of disease throughout a population.

and kidney failure. It did not take many of the bacteria to make people ill. The first known outbreaks of *E. coli* O157:H7 occurred in 1982, when people in Oregon and Michigan became ill after eating undercooked fast-food hamburgers.

Some "new" foodborne diseases may not be new at all. Scientists have simply gotten better at identifying old enemies. In 1977, Martin Skirrow reported isolating a type of bacterium from just over 7 percent of patients with diarrhea.[12] Skirrow suspected they had become ill after eating or handling infected chickens. Scientists had known for many years that this bacterium, *Campylobacter jejuni*, could cause disease in sheep and cattle, but had never before linked it to human disease. In truth, *C. jejuni* has probably been a leading cause of foodborne illness for many years, but it is hard to isolate in the laboratory and so remained undiscovered. Today, *C. jejuni* is recognized as a leading cause of foodborne illness in the United States.

Finally, government funding for monitoring infectious disease had been severely cut back, mostly at the state and local levels. In 1994, twelve states had no employees to monitor foodborne disease outbreaks. Experts now believe that the 1992–1993 Jack in the Box outbreak could have been contained earlier if there had been a better system of monitoring foodborne diseases.[13]

# 3

# How Our Bodies Fight Back

**F**ood is not just fuel for our bodies. In many ways, it is one of the great pleasures of life. It comes as a shock to realize that the food we love and trust—raspberries and whipped cream, or a simple egg, fried sunny-side up—can sometimes carry harmful microbes. How do they get there? And how do our bodies fight back?

Some pathogens, such as the bacterium that causes botulism, lead double lives. In the soil or water, it lies dormant, protected from the environment by a tough coat, or spore. The spore form of the *Clostridium botulinum* bacterium may cling to potatoes, green beans, and even seafood. For most people, the dormant form of the bacterium is not harmful (although it can cause disease in infants).

*C. botulinum* becomes active, and therefore dangerous, only under oxygen-free conditions. The active bacterium produces a potent toxin that attacks the nervous system. The canning process, by removing nearly all the oxygen from the container, creates an ideal environment for the active form of *C. botulinum*—unless the container and its contents are heated to 121°C (250°F) for a sufficient period. The oxygen-free interiors of preserved meats would also provide an ideal environment for the actively growing bacterium if it were not for the addition of salt and nitrates. Both inhibit the growth of *C. botulinum*.

# Fecal Contaminants

Many other foodborne pathogens make their homes in the gastrointestinal tracts of animals. The organisms often are not harmful to the animals, even though they cause disease in humans. Sometimes humans who have been infected with a microbe, from an animal or another human, continue to harbor it within their bodies, even after they have recovered. Feces from such a person, called a carrier, may be teeming with these microbes. If the carrier's feces then contaminate food, the microbes can hitch a free ride into the gastrointestinal tract of another victim.

One of the most infamous and tragic carriers of disease was an Irish immigrant to the United States, Mary Mallon. In the early 1900s, Mary was a cook at several well-to-do homes in and around New York City. Although she did not know it, she was also a healthy carrier of *Salmonella typhi*. Mary unwittingly infected more than twenty people through the food she prepared. She became known as Typhoid Mary.

Many of the microbes that cause foodborne infections, including *S. typhi,* can also be transmitted directly from one person to another. The *Shigella* bacterium, for example, is spread through human feces. It can be transmitted through fecal contamination of food or, as is often the case, in places such as day care centers where caregivers diaper many children. Because babies and children often put their hands into their mouths, they can easily pick up microbes from their surroundings.

The presence of feces on food, though not an appealing idea, is common. During the process of slaughtering animals, their intestines may break open, allowing feces to contaminate the surface of the meat. Even if there are no visible feces on the meat, the surface is inevitably covered by an invisible film of microbes. It is impossible for even the most scrupulously clean slaughterhouse to produce beef carcasses that are completely germ-free.

Chicken carcasses can become contaminated in the same way, with an added twist: After the birds are slaughtered, removed of feathers, cleaned, and degutted, they are put into a large cold-water bath. Although the water contains chlorine, it is not enough to kill all the bacteria. The water becomes a kind of "bacteria soup," spreading the microbes throughout the bath. Water absorbed by the chickens can be loaded with bacteria.[1]

It is not just meat that can become contaminated with feces. Raw or insufficiently processed animal sewage may be used to fertilize fruit and vegetable crops. Windfall apples—

those that fall off the tree, onto the ground, and are often used to make apple cider—may become contaminated with bird droppings or bits of cow manure from a nearby pasture.

Infected food handlers—from field-workers to the person flipping the burgers at a local fast-food restaurant—can transmit pathogens if they do not wash their hands thoroughly after using the toilet. A lot of potential pathogens can hide under just one dirty fingernail!

## How We Become Sick

Doctors classify foodborne diseases into two categories, according to what causes them. The first category is called food poisoning, or intoxication. In this case, it is the toxins produced by microbes growing in the food that make us sick, not the microbes themselves. The contaminating microbes may even be dead by the time we eat them. The important thing is that their toxins remain. It usually does not take long—a few hours or even minutes—for a victim of food poisoning to feel ill, especially if there was a lot of toxin present in the contaminated food. The most common food-poisoning bacteria, *Staphylococcus aureus* and *Clostridium perfringens*, cause fairly mild and short-lived symptoms (nausea, vomiting, and diarrhea). Botulism is the most severe type of food poisoning. Unlike the *S. aureus* and *C. perfringens* toxins, which remain within the gastrointestinal system, the botulism toxin passes through the intestinal wall and affects the nervous system.

In the slaughterhouse, workers clean and inspect beef carcasses for accidental contamination.

The second category of foodborne diseases consists of food infections, which occur when we eat food contaminated with living pathogens that grow and multiply inside our bodies. They may also produce toxins that make us ill, but they do so in our bodies. Some, like *Campylobacter* and *E. coli*, like to live in the intestine. They do not migrate to other organs. Other foodborne microbes use the gastrointestinal system as a gateway to the rest of the body. *Salmonella typhi* causes typhoid fever when it enters the bloodstream and spreads throughout the body. The hepatitis A virus migrates to the liver.

## Our Natural Defenses

Imagine for a moment that you just ate that fateful bite of food contaminated with disease-causing microbes or toxins. At this point, you may not know that you have eaten contaminated food—it often tastes, smells, and looks okay. As you chew your food, it is mixed with saliva. Some potential disease-causing microbes never make it past this point; many are killed or inactivated by enzymes in the saliva. Food containing large amounts of bacterial toxins may produce feelings of irritation, burning, or tingling sensations at the back of the throat.

Next, the food travels down the esophagus to the stomach, a very acidic environment. The acid not only helps digest food but can kill many pathogens as well. Some do manage to survive. Food high in fat can coat and protect pathogens as they pass through the stomach. Few microbes do their dirty work here, although some bacterial toxins, including the type produced by the common *S. aureus*, can irritate the stomach and induce vomiting.

Microbes that survive the stomach move on to the small intestine. Here, they face bile acids and digestive enzymes. The intestine's wavelike movements constantly move them about. Patches of immune cells lining the small intestine may detect and help turn away or inactivate potential invaders. As the microbes move farther down the small intestine and into the large intestine, they must compete for space and nutrients with the more than four hundred species of resident bacteria, or normal flora—all 100 trillion of them. In addition to crowding out harmful bacteria, the normal flora help digest food and produce some vitamins.

## When Our Bodies Lose

Nevertheless, some pathogens do manage to colonize the small and large intestines. They often have special proteins that enable them to cling to the intestinal walls. Once established, they may multiply and produce toxins that result in watery diarrhea and dehydration. The bacterium that causes cholera, *Vibrio cholerae*, is very good at this. Other bacteria, most notably the *E. coli* O157:H7 that nearly killed Brianne Kiner, may produce toxins that cling to receptors in the intestine, kidney, and central nervous system, eventually causing cell death.

## Who Is at Risk?

Given our impressive defenses against foodborne pathogens, why do we get sick at all? Sometimes, if the level of microbial

# Are Microbes, Not Stress, the Cause of Ulcers?

Scientists have recently found an enterprising type of bacterium, called *Helicobacter pylori,* that not only tolerates but thrives in the stomach's acidic environment. Although many people believe that emotional stress causes ulcers, it is this bacterium, not stress, that is probably responsible for most cases of stomach ulcers.[2]

contamination is high enough, our defenses are simply overwhelmed. In other cases, our bodies are in a condition that makes it easier for pathogens to survive. For instance, otherwise healthy adults may make life easier for disease-causing microbes by taking antacids, which neutralize the stomach acids. Antibiotics taken for another illness can kill off significant numbers of our normal intestinal bacteria. Simple lack of competition for space and nutrients makes it easier for invading pathogens to colonize the intestinal wall. Pregnant women are at special risk for infections from a bacterium called *Listeria monocytogenes,* which can cause spontaneous abortions or stillbirths.

Babies under the age of one year are at particular risk for foodborne diseases because their immune systems are under-developed and their intestines are not yet fully colonized by normal flora.

The elderly, whose immune systems are not as vigorous as they once were, are another high-risk population. Malnutrition, mental stress, and general poor health all cause cells in our bodies to produce chemical messengers that reduce the effectiveness of the immune system. Persons with AIDS, or those who have had an organ transplant or chemotherapy, often have poorly functioning immune systems.

# 4

# A Gallery of Microbes

**D**r. Charles Onufer woke up one cold November morning feeling as though he were coming down with the flu. He felt cold, achy, and lousy. Onufer, a pediatrician, did not feel like going to work, but he had just returned from a ten-day business trip and had a lot of catching up to do. By the time he got home from work, he had a fever and the chills. That evening, he had watery diarrhea. By the fourth day of this misery, he became dehydrated and was admitted into the hospital. Onufer was soon well enough to go home, but his nightmare was only beginning.

Ten days after he first became ill, he had trouble raising his arms. The next day, he could not get up from his seat at the breakfast table. Onufer knew that he had to see his doctor. With his wife's assistance, Onufer got ready to go. "I walked through the kitchen with my winter coat on, took another step, and collapsed on the floor," said Onufer. "I was paralyzed from the neck down. It hit me like a bolt of lightning."[1]

Onufer had Guillain-Barré syndrome (GBS), a paralysis often triggered by a respiratory or gastrointestinal infection. Now that vaccination has nearly eradicated polio, GBS is the leading cause of acute paralysis in the United States. Dr. Onufer's original illness had been caused by *Campylobacter jejuni*, one of the most common triggers of GBS. Onufer suspects that he picked up the bug from undercooked chicken, a common vehicle for this pathogen. Onufer liked chicken and ate it frequently.

Dr. Onufer was one of the "lucky" ones—he gradually regained the use of his muscles, and after four weeks in the hospital, he was home again. Three months later, Onufer's arms and legs were still weak, but he continued to improve . . . slowly.

## Campylobacter

*Campylobacter jejuni* belongs to a rogues' gallery of bacteria, viruses, and protozoa that are of special concern to health officials today. *C. jejuni* was not recognized as a human pathogen until the late 1970s.[2] Nonetheless, experts estimate that it makes 2 to 4 million Americans sick and is responsible for up to one thousand deaths each year.

The rod-shaped bacteria are carried in the guts of healthy cattle, chickens, birds, dogs, and even flies. A recent *Consumer Reports* survey showed that 630 out of 1,000 fresh whole chickens in supermarkets across the country carried *C. jejuni*.[3]

Other major sources of *Campylobacter* are unpasteurized milk and unchlorinated water.

If not killed by heat (poultry should be cooked to a temperature of 82°C, or 180°F), as few as four hundred to five hundred *C. jejuni* bugs may cause illness—a number that could easily be contained in one drop of uncooked chicken juice.[4] The bacteria make their way to the victim's small intestine, where they are thought to produce a toxin. Most people who get a *Campylobacter* infection, called campylobacteriosis, get diarrhea, fever, abdominal cramps, and nausea two to four days after they ate food contaminated with the microbe. They recover in about a week. About 10 percent of *Campylobacter* victims may suffer serious, long-term complications, including arthritis and Guillain-Barré syndrome.

## Salmonella

*Salmonella* is the name of a whole family of microbes that cause an estimated 2 to 4 million infections every year. *Salmonella* infections, or salmonellosis, have increased dramatically in the last two decades.[5] The *Salmonella* strains that cause typhoid fever and a related disease may kill up to 10 percent of their victims, but these strains are relatively rare.

Most forms of salmonellosis have a fatality rate of less than one percent. Many animals, especially poultry and pigs, harbor *Salmonella* in their intestines. The microbe may turn up in raw meats, poultry, eggs, milk and dairy products, and fish. The same *Consumer Reports* survey that looked at *Campylobacter*

Chickens may be carriers of the *Salmonella* bacteria.

in supermarket chickens also found that 16 percent of the chickens were contaminated with *Salmonella*.[6]

In the 1990s, another member of the family, *S. typhimurium*, emerged as a major health problem—first in the United Kingdom, and later in the United States. One major strain, *S. typhimurium* DT 104, is of special concern because it is resistant to several antibiotics.

It takes very few *Salmonella* bacteria to cause disease—as few as fifteen to twenty, depending on the age and health of the host and the strain of the bacteria.[7] They can invade the small intestine, where they produce a toxin. The symptoms, which include diarrhea, vomiting, abdominal cramps, chills, fever, and headache, usually begin six to forty-eight hours after

41

exposure. These symptoms usually clear up in one to six weeks, but a few patients go on to develop a kind of arthritis. Occasionally, the microbe can invade the bloodstream and colonize other organs.

## *Escherichia coli*

*Escherichia coli* is a large family of bacteria. Although most strains of *E. coli* are harmless and live in the intestines of healthy humans and animals, a few can cause disease. Some pathogenic strains of *E. coli* cause what is commonly known as traveler's diarrhea, or Montezuma's revenge. They are common in developing countries where inadequate sanitation may lead to contamination of foods. In most cases, the disease clears up in a few days. Some strains can cause serious, long-lasting diarrhea in infants. Untreated, the infections can lead to severe dehydration and even death.

E. coli O157:H7 is an especially bad member of the family. It is a major cause of bloody and nonbloody diarrhea in the

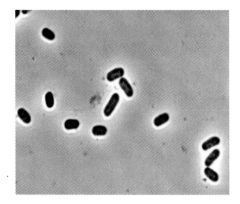

Scientists believe that learning more about the structure and function of disease-causing microbes, including *E. coli* O157:H7 pictured here, will help us find ways to fight foodborne disease.

United States, causing as many as 20,000 illnesses and 250 deaths every year.[8]

*E. coli* O157:H7 lives in the intestines of healthy cattle. If meat becomes contaminated during slaughter, the microbe can be thoroughly mixed into the beef when it is ground into hamburger. Bacteria present on a cow's udder may find its way into raw milk. Raw apple juice pressed from feces-contaminated apples, and lettuce grown in a field near a cow pasture, have also caused recent *E. coli* O157:H7 outbreaks in the United States.[9]

As few as ten *E. coli* O157:H7 bacteria may be all that is necessary to cause disease.[10] Once inside the gut, they release large amounts of a potent toxin that causes severe damage to the lining of the intestine. The symptoms usually begin with severe abdominal cramps and watery diarrhea that soon becomes very bloody. In most cases, the disease clears up in five to ten days. In some people, especially children or the elderly, an *E. coli* O157:H7 infection can cause hemolytic uremic syndrome, a life-threatening condition in which the red blood cells are destroyed and the kidneys fail.

## *Vibrio*

Bacteria of the *Vibrio* genus thrive in warm marine waters where seafood is often harvested. Raw or undercooked shellfish can carry the organisms to the table. In the United States, *Vibrio* bacteria flourish in the waters off the Gulf Coast states in the summer and early fall.

The organism that causes cholera, *Vibrio cholerae,* is generally waterborne and spread by poor sanitation. It can also be transmitted when people eat raw shellfish harvested from beds contaminated with human sewage. Although there have been fewer than eighty proven cases of cholera reported in the United States since 1973, there was a cholera epidemic in Peru in 1991, spread at least in part by raw or undercooked seafood. The epidemic reached other South American and Central American countries, causing more than 340,000 illnesses and 3,600 deaths.

*V. cholerae* attaches to the small intestine and produces a toxin that causes abdominal cramps, nausea, vomiting, and diarrhea, often severe. Death can occur if the victim does not receive medical treatment aimed at preventing dehydration.

More common in the United States is *V. parahaemolyticus.* The microbe attaches itself to the small intestine and releases a toxin. The symptoms of the illness are diarrhea, abdominal cramps, nausea, vomiting, headache, fever, and chills. Fortunately, the illness is usually relatively mild and lasts only one to seven days.

In the 1970s, a particularly nasty member of the *Vibrio* genus, *V. vulnificus,* raised its ugly head. In healthy people, *V. vulnificus* causes a disease similar to that caused by *V. parahaemolyticus.* People with diabetes, AIDS, liver disease, or leukemia, or those who take drugs that suppress the immune system, may develop a more serious disease. This disease, called primary septicemia, occurs when the bacteria enter the bloodstream. It can cause blistering skin lesions, fever, chills,

Although raw fish may carry disease-causing parasites, most sushi chefs in reputable restaurants are skilled at detecting contaminated fish.

and decreased blood pressure (septic shock), rapidly followed by death in over half the cases. Although *V. vulnificus* causes very serious illness for high-risk groups of people, it is not common: Only three hundred cases of infection were reported in the Gulf Coast states between 1988 and 1995.[11]

## *Listeria monocytogenes*

*Listeria monocytogenes* is a whip-tailed bacterium that lives in the intestine of many animals. A fairly hardy organism, *L. monocytogenes* can also be found in the soil and in water. Vegetables can become contaminated from the soil or from manure used as fertilizer. It grows rapidly in refrigerated foods. The most common foods contaminated with *L. monocytogenes* are raw or improperly pasteurized milk, soft cheeses, ice cream, and processed foods such as coleslaw and pâté.

*L. monocytogenes* is such a common microbe that it probably contaminates food fairly often. Yet most healthy people do not get sick if they eat food containing the microbe. The bacteria can cause life-threatening disease, however, in pregnant women, newborn babies, and adults with weakened immune systems. In the United States, an estimated 1,850 people become seriously ill with listeriosis, the disease caused by the microbe.[12] Of these, about 425 die. Pregnant women are twenty times more likely to get listeriosis than other healthy adults, perhaps because their immune systems are less vigorous than usual.[13]

Listeriosis usually begins with flulike symptoms: fever, achy muscles, and sometimes nausea or diarrhea. Trouble begins if the infection spreads to the blood, nervous system, or in pregnant women, the placenta or fetus. It can cause meningitis in the woman (a serious infection around the spine), abortion, or stillbirth. Infants who are born with listeriosis (because their mothers were infected during pregnancy) often have trouble breathing, refuse to drink, and vomit.

## *Staphylococcus aureus*

*Staphylococcus aureus*, like the harmless strains of *E. coli* that live in our guts, is actually part of our normal intestinal contents. It also lives on our skin, in infected cuts and pimples, and in our noses and throats. It becomes a problem when people spread it from their hands to the food they themselves or others eat. *S. aureus* multiplies rapidly and produces a toxin in food held at room temperature. It is thought to cause more than 1.5 million cases of illness, often called staph food poisoning, each year. The most common foods associated with staph poisoning are those that require a lot of handling: egg, potato, chicken, and pasta salads; sandwich fillings; and bakery products such as cream-filled pastries and cream pies.

Although cooking kills the bacteria, their toxin is very resistant to heat, refrigeration, and freezing. It induces nausea, vomiting, and diarrhea, usually two to four hours after eating toxin-contaminated food. The illness lasts for one to two days and is rarely fatal.

47

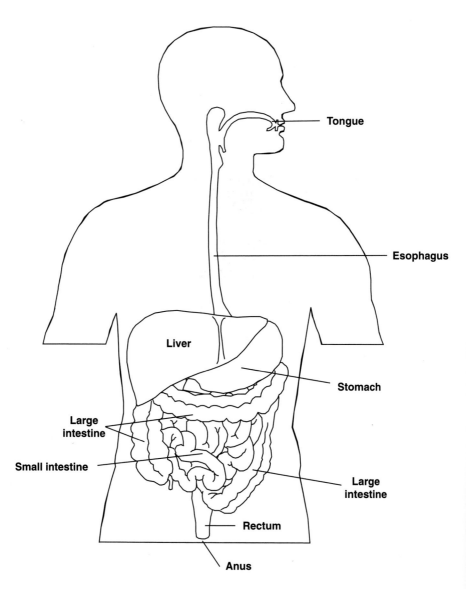

Foodborne diseases make us sick when disease-causing microbes enter our gastrointestinal tracts.

# Clostridium

The *Clostridium botulinum* bacterium is not a common cause of foodborne disease but can cause a disease called botulism that becomes life-threatening if it is not treated immediately. *C. botulinum* bacteria are widespread in nature: They occur in soil, at the bottom of streams, lakes, and coastal waters, and occasionally in some fish and shellfish. The bacteria grow only where there is little or no oxygen. If the conditions are not right, they become dormant, protected by a tough spore. Under the right conditions—as in canned food that has not been heated to a high enough temperature—the spores germinate, or become actively growing bacteria. As they grow, they produce a very potent toxin. The toxin is absorbed through the intestines and into the blood. Eventually it attaches to the nerves and causes double vision, droopy eyelids, and trouble with speaking, breathing, and swallowing. Without treatment, the victim may suffocate.

A member of the same family of bacteria, *Clostridium perfringens* is the cause of one of the most commonly reported foodborne illnesses in the United States. The CDC estimates that about ten thousand cases of *C. perfringens* poisoning occur each year. Like *C. botulinum*, spores of *C. perfringens* are common in the environment. They are frequently isolated from the intestines of humans and animals as well.

Thorough cooking will destroy the spores, but if a few survive, they multiply rapidly as food cools to room temperature. *C. perfringens* is called the "food service germ" because it occurs most often in food served in quantity and left for long periods on a warming table or at room temperature. Meats and gravy are the most common vehicles. Once in the gut, the bacteria produce a toxin that causes abdominal pain, diarrhea, and gas for about a day.

## Parasitic Protozoa

*Cryptosporidium parvum* and *Cyclospora cayetanensis* are single-celled parasites, called protozoa. *Cryptosporidium,* about half the size of a red blood cell, infects many livestock and wild animals. A person can become infected by drinking water or eating raw or undercooked food contaminated with feces containing *Cryptosporidium* oocysts. Oocysts are the egglike forms of the parasite.

Cryptosporidiosis became a household word in 1993 when four hundred thousand people in Milwaukee, Wisconsin, became ill with diarrhea after their drinking water supply was contaminated with the parasite. Other cryptosporidiosis outbreaks have been associated with raw apple cider and raw milk.

Symptoms—usually watery diarrhea, headache, cramps, nausea, vomiting, and fever—may appear two to ten days after infection. For most people, the disease lasts one to two weeks. For others, especially those with AIDS, the disease may continue and become life-threatening.

The *Cyclospora* protozoan, like *Cryptosporidium,* is spread through water or food contaminated with infected feces. It is not known whether animals can be infected and can then spread *Cyclospora.* The parasite infects the small intestine and causes watery diarrhea, loss of appetite, gas, stomach cramps, nausea, vomiting, fever, and fatigue. *Cyclospora* infection was once considered a hazard of travel in developing countries, but with increased international trade of fruits and vegetables it has become a worldwide problem. Pathogens once considered exotic are sometimes imported along with produce from developing countries.

## Viruses

Experts estimate that Norwalk and Norwalk-like viruses cause nearly 65 percent of the cases of nonbacterial gastroenteritis in the United States. These viruses are transmitted when food or water is contaminated with human feces. Salads, for example, are commonly contaminated when food handlers do not wash their hands well after using the bathroom. Other outbreaks of Norwalk virus have been traced to the practice of dumping human sewage into the ocean. Shellfish such as oysters and clams, being filter feeders, readily pick up the virus shed in human stools.

The symptoms of a Norwalk virus are nausea, vomiting, diarrhea, and abdominal pain. They usually begin twelve to forty-eight hours after infection, and last twelve to sixty days. The illness is usually mild, with no known associated deaths.

The hepatitis A virus, like the viruses in the Norwalk family, can be transmitted from one person to another through food contaminated with human feces. About 22,700 cases of hepatitis A are reported each year in the United States. About 7 percent of those cases are transmitted through food or water (most other cases are transmitted through person-to-person contact).[14] Cold cuts and sandwiches, fruits and fruit juices, milk and milk products, salads, shellfish, and even iced drinks have all been found to transfer hepatitis A. Hepatitis A outbreaks are common in institutions, crowded housing projects, and prisons.

The virus usually causes symptoms ten to fifty days after infecting its host. Many hepatitis A infections cause no symptoms at all, and when symptoms do occur, they are usually mild and last one to two weeks. The symptoms of hepatitis A infection are fever, nausea, loss of appetite, abdominal discomfort, and jaundice (a yellowish discoloration of the skin caused by bile deposits). Occasionally, the illness is severe and lasts several months, but very few of the reported cases are fatal.

## Mad Cow Disease: A Threat to Humans?

In 1986, a few British dairy farmers noticed that some of their good-natured cattle became aggressive and nervous, and over time began to stagger and stumble. The disease, which became popularly known as "mad cow disease," soon reached epidemic proportions in Britain. As of September 1998, there had been more than 170,000 confirmed cases in British cattle.[15]

The disease is formally called bovine spongiform encephalopathy (BSE), so named because the brains of the affected cows look like sponges—full of holes. BSE resembles a disease in sheep, called scrapie, which has been present in England for at least two hundred years. Researchers believe the scrapie agent was transferred to cattle when the butchered sheep's leftover parts—called offal—were processed and added to cattle feed as protein supplements. In 1991, the British government started strictly enforcing a ban on protein supplements containing cattle and sheep offal.

The agent is apparently not a bacterium, virus, or parasite. The most popular theory holds that it is a mutant protein called a prion. The agent can withstand high temperatures and chemical disinfectants.

In 1996, British doctors began to notice an unusual cluster of cases of a disease similar to BSE, Creutzfeld-Jacob disease (CJD), in people. Classical CJD is a rare disease affecting elderly people. Like BSE, CJD causes brain damage and death. The relative youth of the victims and other differences tipped researchers off to the fact that this new variant of CJD (nvCJD) was unlike classical CJD. British researchers concluded that eating beef infected with BSE most likely caused these cases of nvCJD. Between 1995 and 1997, twenty-three people in Europe died from nvCJD.

Could BSE and nvCJD cross the Atlantic? So far, there is no evidence that they have. The United States banned the importation of British cattle and processed beef in 1989. In June 1997, the Food and Drug Administration prohibited the use of most protein supplements derived from mammals for cows, sheep, and goats. Some experts feel that the ban does not go far enough. It still allows food supplements for chickens, pigs, and pets to contain protein from mammals, even though scientists have found BSE-like diseases in pigs and cats.

# 5

# Diagnosis and Treatment

**C**arrie McGraw, a surgical nurse at a large hospital in the Chicago suburbs, has vivid memories of her first visit to that hospital. She was eleven years old and had terrible nausea and diarrhea. She shared a room with her younger sister, Kimberly, who had been admitted with the same symptoms a few days earlier. "It was scary," she remembers, "and I was really lonely. I was in isolation, because they didn't know what I had and didn't want me to spread anything to the rest of the floor."[1]

Carrie and her sister were given fluids through an intravenous drip to treat their dehydration. The doctors tested their stools for bacteria and found *Salmonella typhimurium*. By this time their older sister, Kelly, was sick as well. She recovered at home. Their mother, who had cared for them while they were sick, eventually came down with a secondary *Salmonella*

54

infection. Mrs. McGraw caught the microbe not from food, but from taking care of her daughters and handling their waste. "It was not a fun two weeks," said Terry McGraw, the girls' father.[2]

All told, more than sixteen thousand people in the upper midwestern United States were confirmed to have been infected with the same antibiotic-resistant strain of *S. typhimurium* that landed Carrie and her sister Kimberly in the hospital. The real number of infections stemming from the 1985 outbreak was probably closer to two hundred thousand, making it the largest *Salmonella* outbreak identified in the United States.[3] (A later *Salmonella* outbreak, traced to nationally distributed ice cream in 1994, affected about 224,000 people.[4]) Investigators traced the first outbreak to two brands of pasteurized 2 percent milk produced by a single dairy plant.

Investigators eventually discovered a design error in a newly automated and computerized processing plant that allowed unpasteurized, contaminated milk to make its way into the pasteurized milk supply.

Carrie never got back into the habit of drinking milk. "It still haunts me," she said. "And since I had it the worst, the doctors told my parents to watch me for signs of arthritis." (Arthritis is one of the long-term side effects of severe *Salmonella* infections.)

## Should I See a Doctor?

Unlike Carrie and her sisters, the great majority of cases of foodborne disease go unreported and undiagnosed. Many choose not to go to the doctor because their illness is fairly mild. Others may lack access to adequate health care. If they do go to the doctor, physicians may not always order the stool cultures necessary to make a diagnosis; many clinical laboratories are not set up to identify the microbial culprit.

According to some experts, however, even seemingly mild cases of foodborne disease merit at least a telephone call to the doctor. "If the illness is truly part of an outbreak, the more cases we find out about, the more likely we are to implicate a specific food item," said Dr. Kate Glynn, a medical epidemiologist at the CDC in Atlanta, Georgia. People who are only mildly ill can still shed organisms in their stool for a few days after they recover, she added. "The physician might point out things like being extra careful with handwashing and food preparation."[5]

## It Must Have Been Something I Ate . . .

Foodborne diseases are caused by a whole gang of different microbial thugs, as described in Chapter 4. There is no one set of symptoms that can describe all of them. Some of the most common signs, however, are vomiting and diarrhea, abdominal cramps, and possibly a fever. *Gastroenteritis* is the term doctors often use to describe this group of symptoms. The misery usually begins one to ninety-six hours after eating contaminated food and can last from twelve to forty-eight hours or more. Of foodborne illness, one of my microbiology professors in college liked to say, "First you feel like you're going to die, and then you wish you could."

At home, the best thing to do when the symptoms begin is to rest and avoid eating or drinking anything for a couple of hours. After two to four hours, begin—slowly, at first—to drink clear liquids. Apple or grape juice, flat ginger ale, broth, and tea are good choices, as are gelatin desserts. Many doctors recommend the sports drinks that supply electrolytes, essential substances such as potassium and sodium. It is important to replace lost fluids and electrolytes so that you do not become dehydrated.

After a day or so, you can begin to eat small portions of bland foods. Bananas, applesauce, toast, saltine crackers, rice, and potatoes are all good choices. Avoid dairy products and greasy foods, which can be difficult to digest.

Unless a doctor specifically recommends them, do not use over-the-counter antidiarrheal remedies for foodborne disease. Diarrhea, miserable as it makes us feel, is our body's way of flushing out the offending microbes. Antidiarrheal medicines could actually prolong the illness. Throughout your illness, and even after you recover, good handwashing is important, especially after using the bathroom (which is good advice anytime!). This is an important step in preventing the spread of the disease to others. Those taking care of the patient should follow the same advice.

There are some symptoms or conditions that should send you to the doctor right away. Dehydration, signaled by light-headedness, faintness, dizziness, and lethargy, is the number one concern. Untreated, it can lead to shock and even death. "Dehydration can develop quite quickly in people who are

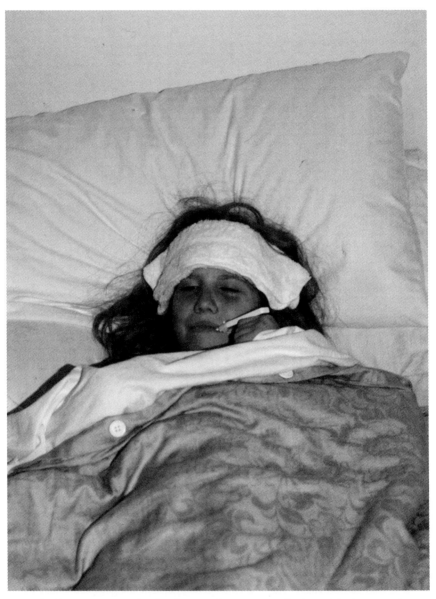

The best treatment for foodborne illness is usually lots of bed rest and plenty of fluids.

unable to absorb or hold down fluids," said Raymond Chung, a doctor who specializes in gastrointestinal and liver diseases at Massachusetts General Hospital in Boston. "A patient who has been unable to hold down fluids for the better portion of a day—say twelve hours or more—is at risk of developing significant dehydration."[6]

Bloody diarrhea should also raise a red flag. Bloody diarrhea implies an invasive bacterial infection of the colon, usually caused by *Salmonella, Shigella, Yersinia, Campylobacter,* or several members of the *E. coli* family, including *E. coli* O157:H7. All are potentially serious infections. It could also be a sign of another, nonbacterial disease altogether.

People whose immune systems are weakened—because of HIV infection, cancer, or chemotherapy—should also see a doctor promptly. Pregnant women, diabetics, people taking steroids, the very young, and the very old are also at risk and should receive prompt medical attention.

## In the Clinic or Hospital

The first thing the doctor is likely to do at the clinic or hospital is a physical exam and history. He or she is likely to ask whether the patient has recently traveled and whether anyone else in the household has been sick. The answers to these and other questions often provide important clues as the doctor is making a diagnosis.

"It is important to assess whether there is abdominal pain or tenderness," said Dr. Chung, "because some of these infections can be associated with tenderness."[7] The doctor will look for signs of jaundice (a yellowish tinge to the eyes and skin caused by bile pigments from the liver), a symptom of hepatitis infections. There may be a rectal exam to look for blood in the stool.

The physician may run a series of blood tests to look for signs of infection and dehydration and send a stool sample to the hospital laboratory. Lab technicians prepare cultures from the stool to detect a range of bacteria and parasites. They can also test for white blood cells, an indication of infection.

If the doctor suspects food poisoning caused by bacterial toxins (*Staphylococcus aureus, Clostridium perfringens,* and *Bacillus cereus* are the usual suspects), he or she will usually "just do detective work through the history."[8] These bacteria usually cause symptoms within hours of eating tainted food and usually do not cause serious illness.

As for treatment, getting fluids into the patient, whether by mouth or through an intravenous drip, is usually the first order of business. After the lab results come back and the doctor knows the identity of the pathogen, antibiotics may be prescribed. Most healthy people, however, have immune systems that can handle the infection, Dr. Chung said. "Antibiotics should be prescribed by doctors," cautioned Dr. Chung. "They shouldn't be taken from parents' or from friends' supplies, and they shouldn't be taken for everything that ails you."[9] The overuse of antibiotics is a serious problem today. Bacteria can change rapidly, and the careless use of antibiotics can actually help create drug-resistant microbes.

# Disease Detectives Nab Microbial Suspect

Kate Glynn at the CDC in Atlanta, Georgia, got a call from the Kansas state health department. They had been investigating a suspected outbreak of *Salmonella* in the Kansas City area for a few weeks. They and their colleagues in the Missouri state health department thought contaminated produce might be to blame, but they needed help. Could she pack her bags tonight and leave for Kansas tomorrow?

Of course she could. An officer in the CDC's Epidemic Intelligence Service (EIS), Dr. Glynn was accustomed to flying off at a moment's notice to investigate suspected outbreaks of foodborne illness.

A doctor who thinks that a patient may have foodborne disease will sometimes send the patient's stools to the laboratory to be screened for disease-causing microbes. Kansas, like many other states, requests that all *Salmonella* isolates be sent to the state health department. A microbiologist at the Missouri state health department noticed that clinical laboratories from the Kansas City area were sending her an unusually large number of a relatively uncommon type of salmonella— *Salmonella* Infantis. Some Kansas City, Kansas, patients had seen doctors just across the river, in Kansas City, Missouri; as a result, their *Salmonella* isolates were forwarded to the Missouri state lab. Soon, *S.* Infantis was joined by another unusual *Salmonella*, *S.* Anatum.

Meanwhile, people continued to get sick. The victims were more likely to be women than men. Many were relatively young—in their twenties or thirties. By the time Dr. Glynn

Courtesy of Partnership for Food Safety Education

To keep food safe from bacteria, follow the above safety guidelines.

and the rest of the EIS team arrived on the scene, more than fifty people in the Kansas City area had become infected with either *S. Infantis* or *S. Anatum*. Nobody had a clue as to what was making them sick.

## Is It an Outbreak?

The team's first question was simple. Is this truly an outbreak? Was the increase in *S. Infantis* and *S. Anatum* isolates real, or was it just a blip on the charts? Had the labs begun using a new test that made it easier to detect *S. Infantis* or *S. Anatum*? Were cases being reported twice?

The team quickly became convinced that the outbreak was real. "In each of these given states, we would only expect about five cases of each of these serotypes in an entire year," said Dr. Glynn. "And yet here we had, ultimately, over one hundred cases in about a two-month period."[10]

The team sat down with eight carefully chosen outbreak victims and asked them about everything they had done in the three days before they got sick. "We tried to find people who might represent special pieces of the puzzle," said Dr. Glynn.[11] The team examined their checkbooks, their credit card slips, their calendars. Where did they eat? What did they eat? Where did they shop for groceries?

They talked with a university student who ate only at the dormitory cafeteria. One elderly woman had some other health problems and so kept very good records of her meals. One young man had been out of town on spring break that week but had brought some food from the area with him on his trip. "We found two coworkers who were both ill," said Dr. Glynn. "The only thing they had in common was eating at one restaurant for lunch; they didn't really do anything else together."[12]

Everyone they interviewed had eaten iceberg lettuce, but that was probably just a coincidence as iceberg lettuce is a very common food. Cheese and chicken seemed to be mentioned often too, but in varied forms. The cheese might have been prepackaged slices of American cheese or shredded mozzarella; the chicken, fast-food patties or roasted.

And then the investigators hit pay dirt. Six out of the eight people they interviewed had eaten alfalfa sprouts, though not all of them realized (or admitted) it. "I would never eat alfalfa sprouts. I hate them," said one person. But that person—and over a hundred others—did in fact eat alfalfa sprouts, an ingredient in many a veggie sandwich and gourmet salad. "What is the probability that six of eight people who really have very little else in common would all have eaten alfalfa sprouts?" asked Dr. Glynn. "We thought that was actually pretty unlikely."[13]

## The Source of the Problem

The EIS team interviewed other people in the area who had come down with the suspicious *Salmonella* infection, as well as others who were completely well. Those people who became infected with either *S.* Infantis or *S.* Anatum were four times more likely to have eaten alfalfa sprouts than those who had not become infected. What is more, the investigators traced the suspicious sprouts to one source: a nearby seed-sprouting plant.

It turned out that the seed-sprouting facility had bought alfalfa seeds from local farmers. Scientists were able to isolate *S. Anatum* from the seeds, and they felt sure that *S. Infantis* was also present. The seeds were grown in fields primarily intended for growing alfalfa hay to feed animals. A small percentage of the seed was harvested and later sold to the sprouters. Birds or other animals passing through the field may have contaminated the seeds; no one really knows. The scientists did determine that the seeds were already contaminated by the time they arrived at the sprouting facility.

In the end, over one hundred people were hospitalized or at the very least missed days of work or school. The seed-sprouting facility had to recall its alfalfa sprouts, find a new source for its seeds, and shut down its plant while it disinfected the building.

It is vital, said Dr. Glynn, to keep an open mind during outbreak investigations. "The patients may think of the burrito they ate the day before, or an undercooked hamburger," but it is up to the disease detective to ask the right questions, put the pieces together, and find the real culprit. Being an epidemiologist, says Dr. Glynn, is kind of "being like a little terrier. You just do not give up."[14]

# 6

# Prevention

atty Smith was graduating from eighth grade; her sister Sally, from high school. Their family threw a big graduation party for the two of them in their backyard, with a huge spread of food. The party was perfect, and the weather had cooperated by being warm and sunny. Patty's mother had filled a hollowed-out watermelon with a variety of melon balls. "It was out most of the day," Patty recalls, "and as we were cleaning up that evening, Sally said, 'Oh, taste this. Fermented melon.'"

Knowing that the fermentation process turns naturally occurring sugars into alcohol, the girls gorged on the melon, hoping to get tipsy. "We ate tons of it," Patty said. Later that night, happy but still sober, the girls fell asleep in their shared bedroom.

"About three in the morning," Patty laughs, "we both sat upright and looked at each other in horror. Holding our mouths, we ran to different bathrooms and vomited." Fortunately, their illness was short-lived. The next day the girls were better—and wiser. "We figured that it had to be the watermelon," Patty concluded. "I never did that again."[1]

Patty and Sally were probably right. Those melon balls had not fermented but provided an ideal breeding ground for bacteria. The microbes could have come from their mother's hands as she prepared the dish, the curious fingers of young partygoers, an untimely sneeze, or a wandering fly. Whatever the source of contamination, the fruit was probably swimming with microbes by the end of the long, warm day. Patty and Sally could have prevented their three A.M. dash to the bathroom if they had just remembered one of the first rules of food safety: Keep hot foods hot and cold foods cold.

Government officials say that the United States has the safest food supply in the world. That may be true, but the unpleasant fact remains that the food we buy in the supermarket may very well be contaminated with disease-causing organisms. Microbes are everywhere, and there are many points, from the farm to the table, where contamination can occur. There is simply no such thing as germ-free food. You cannot always prevent foodborne disease, but you can go a long way by following some important food safety rules at the supermarket, at home, and in the restaurant.

## At the Supermarket

Food safety begins at the supermarket. Shop for packaged and canned foods first. Do not buy food in cans that are dented or bulging, or have rust around the seams. Likewise, do not buy food in jars that are cracked or have loose or bulging lids. Any of these products may be contaminated, especially with *Clostridium botulinum,* which thrives in airless environments.

Check the expiration dates on canned foods and dairy products such as milk, cottage cheese, and yogurt. Buy refrigerated, uncracked eggs. Pick up frozen and refrigerated foods such as meat, poultry, or fish last. Too much time at room temperature in your shopping cart may give microbes on the foods the edge they need to grow. Use a plastic bag to prevent raw juices from dripping onto other food in your shopping cart. Make sure that frozen foods are solid, not soft. If you cannot take your groceries home right away, it is a good idea to carry an ice chest in the car for the cold and frozen foods.

Think about *what* you buy as well. The U.S. Department of Agriculture advises against purchasing fresh, prestuffed whole poultry. If you want to stuff a bird, do it yourself at home just before cooking it.

## In the Kitchen

The first rule of food safety in the kitchen is simple: Keep food clean. Wash your hands thoroughly with hot, soapy water before you handle food and again after handling raw meat or poultry. If you are on a picnic or camping trip, be sure to bring along plenty of premoistened wipes. Be sure that any cut or sore on your hands is covered; if you have an infection, it is better to stay out of the kitchen altogether.

Thoroughly wash fruits and vegetables, even peeled baby carrots or prepackaged lettuce mixes labeled "prewashed." Wash the rind of produce such as cantaloupes and lemons before cutting into them. You do not eat the rind, of course, but bacteria from the outside can be transferred to the inside when you cut into the fruit.

Canned food can be contaminated in the same way; use warm water and soap to wash the lids before opening to prevent

Wash all fruits and vegetables carefully, especially produce that is not going to be cooked.

dirt and bacteria from getting into the food. Wash the blade of the can opener after each use.

Keep the food preparation area clean, and prevent cross-contamination. One of the most common examples of cross-contamination occurs when the cook cuts up a chicken on a cutting board and then uses the unwashed cutting board to prepare a salad. The salad ingredients can easily pick up microbes left from the chicken juices on the cutting board. Any utensil, plate, or cutting board that has touched raw meat, poultry, or fish must be washed thoroughly before being used for anything else. If you take hamburger patties out to the grill on one plate, do not put them on the same plate after you finish cooking the burgers—an all too common mistake! Use one spatula to transfer the burgers to the grill, and a second one to take them off the grill.

Use smooth cutting boards made from hard wood or plastic, and wash them with hot water, soap, and a scrub brush after use. Some people prefer to use one cutting board for meats and another for vegetables. They can be further sanitized in the dishwasher or by rinsing with a dilute solution of two teaspoons of bleach in a quart of water.

Dishrags and sponges may actually spread bacteria in the kitchen. One group of researchers found that most of the dishrags and sponges in home kitchens harbor large numbers of potentially disease-causing bacteria.[2] Sponges and dishrags stay moist for long periods of time and, if they are used to mop up kitchen spills, provide a constant supply of food for microbial critters. Microbes can even colonize stainless steel, according to another researcher. Metal surfaces that appear smooth to you or me are "full of all kinds of nooks and crannies, canyons, gullies, and hills," says Edmund A. Zottola of the University of Minnesota. "Whenever bacteria find a site harboring moisture and food," Zottola adds, "they will set up housekeeping and grow."[3]

Fortunately, even the most tenacious invaders can be banished by a good scrubbing, followed by a rinse with dilute bleach. Replace kitchen sponges and wash dishrags frequently.

This may go without saying, but keep pets off of tables and kitchen counters. Those adorable cat paws were standing in kitty litter not so very long ago.

The second rule of kitchen food safety: Keep cold foods cold (40°F or lower) and hot foods hot (140°F or higher). Most bacteria multiply rapidly between 40°F and 140°F—the range that food safety experts call the "danger zone." Never thaw frozen chicken or meat at room temperature. Thaw them in the refrigerator for a day or two, or keep them submerged in cold, flowing water. Defrosting in the microwave is safe, too, as long as you follow the manufacturer's instructions.

## Proper Cooking Techniques Kill Microbes

Cook food thoroughly. Do not rely on the color inside—some ground beef may turn brown before it is thoroughly cooked. Instead, use a thermometer. An "instant-read" thermometer inserted into the thickest part of the meat will register the correct temperature in about fifteen seconds. Whole cuts of beef, lamb, and veal should be cooked to 145°F; while ground

Learn how to use a meat thermometer, and cook all meat and poultry to the proper temperatures.

beef and all pork should be cooked to 160°F. Poultry must be cooked to 180°F. Hamburger should not be pink inside, and the juices of poultry should run clear.

Cook fish until it flakes with a fork. Well-cooked shrimp is pinkish and opaque. Sauté, steam, or boil oysters until plump, about five minutes. Steam clams and mussels five to ten minutes or until the shells open (discard any with unopened shells).

Raw or undercooked eggs are responsible for about 80 percent of *Salmonella enteritidis* outbreaks in which a food source was identified. It is a good idea to cook eggs until both the white and yolk are firm. Eggs fried "over easy" and "sunny-side up" account for almost half the undercooked eggs eaten, according to four recent surveys.[4] Many recipes, including those for cake frosting, Caesar salad, and homemade mayonnaise call for raw or nearly raw eggs. Instead of using raw eggs, use pasteurized egg products, found in the dairy section of many supermarkets.

As for sampling homemade raw cookie dough (some people are so fond of it that they are lucky if they end up with a dozen baked cookies)—do not do it. It is okay to sample the commercially prepared refrigerated cookie dough from the grocery store because it contains pasteurized eggs. (The eggs in cookie-dough ice cream are pasteurized, too.)

If you take a lunch to school or work, it is best to use a small, insulated lunch box. Chill food before packing, or freeze it. Put reusable ice packs on top. To keep hot food really hot—soup, for example—preheat a thermos by pouring boiling water into it, then dump the water out before adding the hot soup.

Do not allow perishable foods to remain at room temperature for more than two hours—less in hot weather. Even if you and your friends are having a great conversation, get up and put that leftover pizza in the refrigerator when you are finished eating.

Cooking or reheating food in the microwave oven is safe, as long as you remember that the microwave oven does not cook foods as evenly as a conventional oven. You should rotate the dish or stir the food halfway through the cooking process.

Cooking bags or lids help hold in the heat and steam, which makes the cooking more even. Many microwave recipes call for a standing time after the food is cooked. Do not be tempted to skip this step! This is an essential part of the cooking process and allows all the food to reach the proper temperature.

## Eating Out

When you are eating out, you have to trust the kitchen crew to follow safe food practices. Suzanne Kiner always makes sure there is soap in the restaurant's bathroom—and uses it before eating. "Whether I'm in a fast-food joint or a fancy restaurant, if the bathroom is out of soap, I ask someone in charge to get some," said Kiner. "And I stand there until they do it."[5] Do not be shy about sending food back to the kitchen if it appears to be undercooked. If your chicken should be hot and it is cool, or if your coleslaw is warm instead of cold, send them back.

Those who are traveling abroad, especially to developing countries, should take extra precautions. If there is any reason to doubt the safety of the water, either have it boiled or drink bottled soda, water, or pasteurized juice. Avoid any uncooked food, other than fruits and vegetables that can be peeled. The traveler's mantra is "Cook it, peel it, or leave it." If there is any doubt, avoid it.

## Food Producers, Processors, and the Government

Of course, the responsibility for safe food is not in the hands (preferably *clean*) of the consumer alone. In some cases,

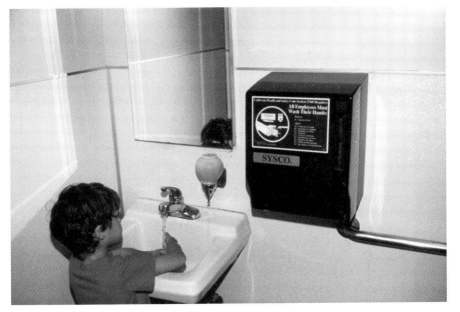

Always wash your hands before eating.

following food safety guidelines—such as washing fresh fruits and vegetables before eating them—may not be enough. Japanese researchers reported at an international conference on infectious diseases that *E. coli* O157:H7 can bury itself below the outer surface of radish sprouts grown in contaminated soil. Even soaking the experimentally contaminated sprouts in a strong disinfectant for ten minutes did not get rid of the bacteria.[6] At that same conference, an official from the Los Angeles Health Department reviewed outbreaks of illness from raspberries tainted with *Cyclospora* and found that the berries had been rinsed in half the cases.[7]

People who are at high risk for a serious foodborne disease, especially those whose immune systems are weakened or who are pregnant, are often well advised to avoid these foods.

It is clear that those who produce and process our food, as well as the government agencies that oversee food safety, share the responsibility of ensuring the safety of our food. The chicken farmer has the responsibility of controlling the spread of pathogens such as *Salmonella* through the flock. The slaughterhouses have the responsibility of turning out the cleanest possible meat and poultry carcasses. Those who process, transport, and sell food have the responsibility of keeping food clean and preventing the spread of foodborne pathogens.

Chapter 8 will examine some of the steps that state and federal regulatory agencies, industry, and food scientists are taking to improve food safety.

# Raw Oysters and Other Risky Foods

I have a weakness for oysters on the half shell. A few years ago, I ordered them at a Seattle restaurant. I was young, healthy, and not pregnant. It was midwinter (shellfish are most likely to carry bacteria in the warm summer months), and I *really* wanted them. They were delicious, but a couple of days later, I got sick. Like most people with foodborne diseases, I did not go to the doctor, but I am fairly sure it was the oysters. Would I eat them again? Probably, but I know I would be taking a chance with getting sick again. I would not do it if I were pregnant, elderly, diabetic, taking antacids, or had a weak immune system or liver disease. I also would not give raw oysters to my children, because their immune systems are not yet mature.

Many people, even some food safety experts, continue to eat risky foods even though they know there is a chance that such foods may harbor disease-causing microbes or parasites. In a *New York Times* article about food safety, Steven Grover, a public health and safety expert with the National Restaurant Association, suggested that "before people indulge in slightly risky culinary behavior they should talk to their physicians about any condition they are being treated for or any medicine they are taking."[8]

The risks people choose to take depend on individual circumstances and tastes. Some food safety experts will eat raw or undercooked eggs but not raw oysters, for example. The risks of using unpasteurized eggs are lower at home than in many restaurants, according to Morris Potter, assistant director for Foodborne Disease at the CDC. Because it is efficient,

The favorite breakfast of many, sausages and eggs, can carry disease-causing microbes if improperly cooked.

restaurants often pool dozens of eggs, a practice that increases the chances for contamination. One pathogen-carrying egg will contaminate the entire batch. "A single raw egg is not as dangerous as eating a raw egg from a pool of raw eggs," said Dr. Potter.[9]

Consider the severity of the disease you might get by eating risky foods. You might be willing to accept the risk of getting a mild case of food poisoning if you really want those raw oysters, but what about becoming infected with *E. coli* O157:H7 if you eat undercooked hamburgers? It is not worth the risk. When you eat undercooked hamburgers, you are not flirting with an upset stomach but with grave illness.

Likewise, most food safety experts advise against drinking unpasteurized milk or juice. U.S. dairies that sell raw milk must undergo a certification process that is supposed to ensure that the farm and milk are clean. The udder of even a healthy cow hosts myriad bacteria, however, many of which can cause disease in humans. One recent British study showed that one fifth of samples of unpasteurized milk bought from grocery stores were contaminated with bacteria, some of them pathogenic. The authors of the study concluded that unpasteurized milk was an "unacceptable risk to public health."[10]

In the same light, pasteurized juice is safer than raw juice. *E. coli* O157:H7 and *Salmonella* outbreaks have been traced to raw juice and cider. If you insist on drinking raw milk or juices, remember that you are taking a risk most food safety experts would not take. And if you are in a high-risk category, forget about it.

# 7

# The High Cost to Society

Six-year-old Alex Donley's idea of a great meal was a hamburger with ketchup. One July day, Alex's burger carried an extra, unwelcome ingredient: *E. coli* O157:H7. Not long after that, Alex began having severe stomach cramps. "So much," his mother said, "that I was up all night with him." Four days later, the red-haired boy was dead. What happened in between, says his mother, was terrifying. He was in agony. His brain swelled, and he began to suffer delusions and tremors. He did not recognize his mother. Mercifully, Alex slipped into a coma before he died. The doctors who performed the autopsy told Nancy and Thomas Donley that Alex could not be an organ donor because most of his organs were completely destroyed by the bacteria's toxin.[1]

Although foodborne illnesses are often referred to in jest as the "collywobbles," the "trots," or "Montezuma's revenge," they are no joke. In the United States alone, microbial pathogens cause an estimated 6.5 to 33 million cases of human illness and up to nine thousand deaths each year.[2]

Most foodborne diseases are mild and do not last very long. Victims usually recover in a few days or, at the most, a few weeks. But many foodborne pathogens can cause chronic and debilitating illness. *Escherichia coli* O157:H7 infection is a leading cause of hemolytic uremic syndrome, the most common cause of acute kidney failure in the United States.[3] Listeriosis can cause miscarriages or result in meningitis in patients with chronic disease.[4] *Salmonella* infections can cause a form of arthritis. And 20 to 40 percent or more of patients with Guillain-Barré syndrome had become infected with *Campylobacter* in the one to three weeks before they got sick.[5]

Foodborne diseases exact a financial cost from society as well. In 1996, there were an estimated 3.3 to 12.4 million cases of foodborne illnesses from just seven microbial pathogens—*Salmonella, Campylobacter jejuni, Escherichia coli* O157:H7, *Listeria monocytogenes, Staphylococcus aureus, Toxoplasma gondii,* and *Clostridium perfringens.* The USDA's Economic Research Service conservatively estimated that the medical costs and loss of productivity at work for these seven foodborne pathogens is between 6.6 and 14.5 billion dollars. The authors of the study point out that the estimate, based only on seven out of the more than forty different foodborne pathogens believed to cause illness, undervalues the true costs of foodborne illness. Not all long-term complications linked to foodborne illness are included in the estimate. Total costs would also increase, they write, "if we include other societal costs, such as pain and suffering, travel to medical care, and lost leisure time."[6]

## A Worldwide Problem

The World Health Organization (WHO) estimates that hundreds of millions of people worldwide suffer from foodborne diseases, with developing countries bearing the brunt of the problem. Each year, there are 1.5 billion episodes of diarrhea in children under the age of five, resulting in 3 million deaths (mainly in developing countries). The WHO estimates that 70 percent of these cases are caused by foodborne pathogens.[7]

Foodborne diseases also contribute to malnutrition, especially in developing countries where children and infants become infected not just once or twice but over and over again. These children cannot grow and develop as they should. Because their immune systems are often weakened, they are more likely to come down with other diseases. The children, according to the WHO's director of the Food Safety and Food Aid program, are "caught in a vicious cycle of malnutrition and infection. Many infants and children do not survive under these circumstances."[8]

Raw fruits and vegetables are good for you, but it is important to wash
your produce thoroughly. It may be contaminated with disease-causing
microbes from the soil or from food handlers.

## Tourism and Trade

Epidemics of foodborne diseases can affect both tourism and trade. Peru's cholera epidemic in 1991 cost that country over 700 million dollars in lost fish and fishery product exports. Many restaurants were closed, and tourism dropped, costing Peru an additional 70 million dollars in the first three months of the epidemic.

Consumers in the United States have come to expect a variety of fresh produce year-round—and we get it, thanks to our global food market. Food imports to the United States have doubled since the 1980s; depending on the season, up to 70 percent of the fruits and vegetables consumed in the United States come from Mexico alone.

There may be a price to pay for the luxury of raspberries in January, however. Outbreaks of foodborne disease linked to imported produce—Guatemalan raspberries, Peruvian carrots, Mexican strawberries and cantaloupe—are on the rise. Imported produce may be no more dangerous than domestically produced fruits and vegetables. Nonetheless, President Clinton has called for a ban on imports on fruits and vegetables from countries that do not meet American food safety standards—a move that at the very least will affect United States foreign trade policies with other countries.

## Personal Losses

Consider, once more, Alex's story. Alex had a friend, also named Alex, who lived down the block. "Just this Christmas, four and a half years after Alex's death, his friend came to our house," remembers Nancy Donley. "He said, 'Can you please tell me where your son is buried?' You see, this boy, after all these years, still has not coped with my Alex's death. He and his family have been in therapy to deal with the loss of his friend. And I guarantee you that all of those dollars spent on therapy, the grief and the heartache are not captured in anyone's statistics on the costs of foodborne illness."[9]

# 8

# New Directions in Food Safety

I t looked as though a bad flu bug was making the rounds in the schools of Marshall, Michigan. Ten-year-old Lindsay Doneth was one of the first children to become ill. She was hospitalized after three days of severe abdominal cramps, vomiting, fever, and splitting headaches. Her liver was so inflamed that it was difficult for her to move. During the six days Lindsay was in the hospital, she lost 10 percent of her body weight.

Over the next four days, hundreds of schoolchildren and a few teachers joined Lindsay in Marshall's small hospital. "The hospital was absolutely overwhelmed with patients," remembered Lindsay's mother, Sue Doneth. "We were told they were making makeshift rooms out of offices."[1]

The "flu bug" that would eventually sicken more than three hundred fifty people in the Marshall area was the hepatitis A virus. The initial victims, some two hundred schoolchildren and teachers, had eaten hepatitis A–contaminated strawberries with their school lunches four weeks earlier. Others became ill through person-to-person contact with those infected with the virus.

The strawberries, investigators found, had been imported from Mexico. In 1996 and 1997, thousands of people became ill after eating Guatemalan raspberries contaminated with *Cyclospora*, a parasite familiar to residents of developing countries but nearly unknown in the United States. The increase in imported foods has strained the United States food safety system, according to Dr. David Kessler, commissioner of the Food and Drug Administration from 1990 through 1997. "We built a system back one hundred years ago that served us very well for a world within our borders," he told *The New York Times*. "We didn't build a system for the global marketplace."[2]

Indeed, the entire United States food safety system has been called into question. The 1992–1993 Jack in the Box *E. coli* O157:H7 outbreak served as a wake-up call to the nation. It was not the first outbreak of foodborne disease, nor was it the largest. But it scared the public, the food industry, and the government because the illness caused by *E. coli* O157:H7 is so severe and sometimes fatal. Its primary victims were children. It was carried on the all-American hamburger. And although proper cooking could have destroyed the pathogen, in the years that followed it found its way into a brand of raw apple cider, lettuce, and sprouts. It was no longer enough to remind consumers to keep hot foods hot and cold foods cold, or to wash their hands and prevent cross-contamination. It was obvious that the United States food safety system would have to undergo a major overhaul.

In January 1997, President Bill Clinton introduced a food safety initiative designed to lower the risk of foodborne disease from both domestic and imported foods. "No parent should have to think twice about the juice that they pour their children at breakfast," said Clinton in a radio address to the nation, "or a hamburger ordered during dinner out."[3]

## Policing the Pathogens

The food safety plan calls for an improved and expanded early-warning system to respond to foodborne outbreaks. In the past, food was usually produced, processed, and eaten locally. The chicken you ate for dinner was likely to have been raised and slaughtered on your own farm or, if you lived in a city, nearby. It was relatively easy to recognize outbreaks of foodborne disease and target the source.

Today, the food on your plate may come from all over the country—or the world. Many outbreaks of foodborne disease go unrecognized simply because their victims are scattered hither and yon. Only some very clever detective work unraveled the mystery of a recent *Salmonella* outbreak involving people in Arizona, Michigan, and Finland. The source: alfalfa sprouts, grown from contaminated seed shipped from the Netherlands.[4]

To help track down the microbial culprits responsible for foodborne outbreaks, scientists at several federal agencies—the CDC, the FDA, and the USDA—and at state and local health departments are developing a national database containing the "fingerprints" of foodborne pathogens. Scientists can create a DNA profile of bacteria—*E. coli* O157:H7, for example—cultured from an ailing patient. You might think that one *E. coli* O157:H7 bacterium looks much like any other. But just as a police detective might use fingerprints to nail one tall, blond-haired, blue-eyed criminal out of a whole lineup of similar-looking suspects, disease detectives can distinguish one substrain of *E. coli* O157:H7 from another by its DNA fingerprints.

Investigators are working to create a permanent, computerized DNA fingerprint library that could be searched by a network of local, state, and federal health agencies. What this means is that if patients from several different states are found to be infected with *E. coli* O157:H7, investigators from each location can report the DNA fingerprints to the database and determine whether there are others that match the profile. Identical fingerprints would tell epidemiologists to look for a common source of infection.

## Monitoring Food Safety

The key to the new initiative is prevention. The meat, poultry, and seafood industries are required to identify the key points at which contamination can occur and come up with a plan to avoid or solve the problem. Government regulators are discussing ways in which a similar plan can be applied to the produce industry. This strategy is known as the HACCP (Hazardous Analysis and Critical Control Points) system.

To some extent, HACCP controls will rely on common-sense measures to prevent foodborne disease. For example, requiring oyster harvesters to use toilets with holding tanks in their boats, instead of dumping their waste into the ocean, is an obvious way to reduce contamination of shallow oyster beds. Other solutions may not be quite so simple. Many food safety experts are concerned with the use of animal manure as fertilizer, for example, especially in the organic food industry.

"'Organic' means that a food is grown in animal manure," said Robert V. Tauxe, chief of the CDC's foodborne and diarrheal diseases branch.[5] Although industry standards say that raw manure should not be applied to food crops within sixty days of harvest, scientists at the University of Georgia have shown that *E. coli* O157:H7 can survive in cattle feces for seventy days, depending on the temperature.[6] "The natural presence and survival of foodborne pathogens in animal manures require a more consistent approach to guarantee that manures do not bring unwanted pathogens with them," wrote Tauxe in a letter to the *Journal of the American Medical Association.*[7]

# Irradiation

One of the most promising technological solutions to the problem of foodborne pathogens is irradiation. Radiation is any kind of energy that moves through space. When we broil or toast food, we are using low-level radiant energy. Food irradiation works by passing X rays, high-energy beams of electrons, or radiation from radioactive cobalt into food. The radiation very effectively kills bacteria and some parasites by fracturing their genetic material. It does not make the food radioactive. One of the most extensively studied food safety technologies in the world, irradiation has long been used to treat food eaten by astronauts and patients with weakened immune systems—people who cannot take a chance on getting a foodborne disease.

"I have been in the food safety business for almost thirty-six years," says Dean Cliver, a professor of population health and reproduction at the University of California–Davis, "and I can't think of anything else that has come along over that span that I thought had as much potential. We could get an awful lot of safety, for very little money, with irradiation." Cliver points out that because irradiation can penetrate muscle, it can kill not just the microbes on the surface of the meat, but parasites such as *Toxoplasma gondii* buried deep within the tissue as well.[8]

Some critics worry that meat processors might come to rely on irradiation to sterilize food processed under filthy conditions. "Our feeling is that the industry should clean up its product as much as possible," says Michael Jacobson, director of the Center for Science in the Public Interest, a consumer advocacy group. "If that fails to provide safe food, then they certainly should provide irradiation. But irradiation should be a last resort."[9] Others worry that irradiation may cause viruses

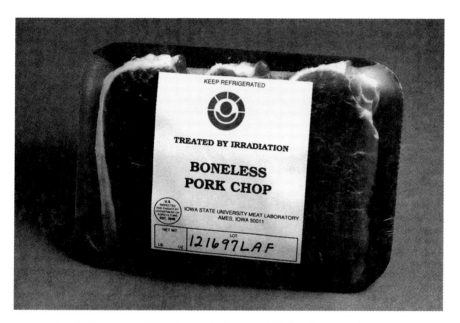

Irradiation is one of the best techniques to kill foodborne pathogens.

and bacterial spores not killed by irradiation to mutate into "superbugs."

These are certainly legitimate concerns. Irradiation is not a magic bullet. It is no substitute for good sanitation and proper cooking. The technology is not as effective against viruses and bacterial spores. It causes leafy vegetables and sprouts to wilt. But as Michael Osterholm and Morris Potter, scientists with the Minnesota Department of Health, point out, the fact that "irradiation pasteurization does not work for every food and every pathogen is poor justification for not applying it for those food/pathogen combinations for which it has been shown to work so well."[10]

Christine Bruhn, director for the Center for Consumer Research at the University of California–Davis, says, "We don't live in a perfect world where we always detect *E. coli* on a processing line, and where everyone washes their hands and cutting boards and cooks meat and poultry to the proper temperature." Food irradiation, she continues, is like an air bag in a car. It offers an extra measure of safety in case of carelessness or an accident.[11]

## Alternatives to Irradiation

There are some alternatives to irradiation on the way. Some meat-processing plants are experimenting with steam pasteurization, in which an entire carcass of beef is blasted with a short burst of steam and then rapidly cooled. The process kills surface pathogens, even those harbored in nooks and crannies, without cooking the meat. The USDA's

Agricultural Research Service is developing a similar method to clean chicken meat.

A promising alternative for produce, including lettuce and sprouts, uses "friendly" lactic acid bacteria. These microbes are the sort normally found in yogurt and fermented foods such as pickles and sauerkraut. Added to refrigerated fruits and vegetables, these bacteria produce substances that may inhibit the growth of *Salmonella, E. coli, Staphylococcus aureus,* and other harmful microbes.[12]

Another alternative to irradiation and traditional heat pasteurization is the use of high-voltage pulses of electricity. In experiments, food is placed between two electrodes and exposed to an extremely short burst of high voltage. The process does not cook or heat the food, but it does dramatically reduce the level of microbes in many foods, including meat, seafood, produce, and baked goods. It is best suited for liquids such as juice, beaten eggs, and even green pea soup. A similar method exposes food to a rapid flash of light about twenty thousand times the intensity of sunlight at sea level.

Japanese consumers can buy jams, jellies, yogurts, and salad dressings that have been pressure-treated, a process that kills all but spore-forming bacteria. The process, which subjects foods to pressures of 50,000 to 100,000 pounds per square inch, tends to squash whole fruits and vegetables, but it works well for foods that do not need to retain any particular form. One company operating on the Mexico-Texas border produces pressure-treated guacamole, and other researchers are testing the technology on orange juice and apple juice.

Although chlorine is the most commonly used disinfectant in the United States today, ozone is actually much faster and more effective at killing bacteria.[13] Ozone is formed in the earth's atmosphere by lightning or high-energy ultraviolet rays. (Ozone is responsible for the fresh, clean smell of the air after a thunderstorm.) Made up of three oxygen atoms (the oxygen molecules we breathe are made up of two oxygen atoms), ozone is a gas that dissolves in water.

Poultry processors are experimenting with using ozone, instead of chlorine, in the water used to chill the chickens. Unlike chlorine, ozone creates no toxic by-products or health hazards when used properly. European countries have long used ozone for purifying air and water and for storing meat, fruit, cheese, and other products.

## Food Safety on the Farm

Food safety begins on the farm, in the feedlot, and in our oceans. We can, in a sense, make our food safer while it is still able to moo, cluck, or swim. Roy Curtiss III, a professor of biology at Washington University in St. Louis, is working with a company called Megan Health to develop a vaccine to inoculate chickens against *Salmonella*. When the vaccine is given to the birds, either as a spray or in their drinking water, newborn chicks, breeder hens, and laying hens develop a lifelong immunity to *Salmonella*.

An *E. coli* O157:H7 vaccine for cattle would seem ideal, but as it turns out, that is a tricky proposition. The bacteria grow in the stomachs of cattle but do not attach to the walls

Food safety begins on the farm and in the fields.

of the stomach or intestine, according to Michael Doyle, director of the Center for Food Safety and Quality Enhancement at the University of Georgia. Even if a cow does develop immunity to *E. coli* O157:H7 or closely related pathogens, referred to collectively as *E. coli* O157, that does not prevent the microbes from living and multiplying in the cow's stomach. The microbes have to be attached to the gut wall in order for immune cells, which are now looking for the particular *E. coli* strain, to get them.

Doyle and his colleagues decided to engage in "germ warfare" instead. He knew that some bacteria produce chemicals that can kill or stop the growth of other bacteria. He and a "very dedicated staff" examined countless samples of manure and intestinal contents from cattle free of *E. coli* O157 and, in the end, isolated several strains of harmless *E. coli* that could inhibit or kill *E. coli* O157:H7.

Using the "good," harmless bacteria, Doyle's group found that they could both prevent infection with *E. coli* O157 in calves and treat an ongoing *E. coli* O157 infection. They will be testing the treatment with feedlot cattle (those animals being fattened up for slaughter) as well.[14]

The food industry needs better ways of testing for pathogens. Testing will not necessarily ensure that every package of hamburger, every raspberry, or every glass of milk is safe, but it can determine whether HACCP measures are working. Poultry and meat slaughterhouses are now required to test for some bacteria. Conventional tests for most microbes take five to seven days. Ideally, food processors would like a testing method that takes only minutes or hours and would allow them to monitor their food as it moves through the production line.

Carl Batt, professor of food science at Cornell University, and his collaborators have developed a sensor that uses antibodies stamped onto a silicon chip. The sensors capture bacteria in a regular, repeating pattern, similar to the UPC bar code used in a supermarket, that can be read using a laser beam.[15]

At the University of Illinois, Hans Blaschek, a food microbiologist, and Zonglin Liu, a visiting professor, have developed a test that can quickly detect small amounts of toxins produced in the early stages of growth of *Clostridium perfringens,* one of the most common causes of foodborne illness. Their method can detect the toxin produced by as few as one thousand cells, far below the million cells required to cause illness.[16]

## Safe Food for All

Irradiation, vaccination, DNA fingerprinting—all may eventually become valuable tools for reducing foodborne disease. But real food safety may depend on our willingness to make difficult changes in the way we think about our food and how it gets to the table.

To meet consumer demand for cheap food, large farms owned by corporations, not small family farmers, are fast becoming the norm. Intensive farming methods make it difficult to check the spread of pathogens throughout a flock or

# Human Vaccines for Foodborne Disease?

In the future, protection against potentially deadly foodborne diseases may be as easy as eating a piece of fruit. Scientists from Cornell University developed a genetically engineered potato containing the gene for a bacterial protein. The protein, which is carried on the surface of a strain of *E. coli* that is a major cause of diarrhea of infants and tourists in developing countries, provokes a strong immune response. Specialized immune cells in the body produce molecules called antibodies that bind to the proteins and help the body get rid of the bacteria.

Scientists from the University of Maryland fed raw chunks of the genetically engineered potatoes to eleven healthy adults three times over the course of three weeks. They found protective antibodies targeting the bacterial protein in the blood and stools of those who ate the modified potatoes.[17]

Another group of scientists, at Thomas Jefferson University in Philadelphia, have created an oral vaccine against botulism. They created a nontoxic version of the *Clostridium botulinum* toxin that survives the tough journey through the gastrointestinal tract and moves into the blood. Although they have yet to test the botulism vaccine in humans, it was effective in protecting mice against botulism poisoning.[18]

herd. The casual use of antibiotics in animal feed has led to new strains of bacteria that are not only resistant to antibiotics but nastier as well.[19]

On a more human level, we need to remedy the fact that those people who harvest, process, and serve our food—from the migrant worker who picks strawberries in the field, to the food handler who shreds lettuce for the salad bar—are often underpaid and lack health insurance. "The food service industry today is one of the most underinsured groups of employed people in the country," says Michael Osterholm, state epidemiologist at the Minnesota Department of Health. "That's important to me as a public health practitioner, because these people often don't seek medical care when they are sick. We've had outbreaks here in Minnesota where management was not even aware of the fact that half of the individuals had diarrhea. None of them had health care, so they didn't leave—they just kept working."[20]

Lastly, there is you—the consumer. Despite all the latest research on food safety, neither the farmer, nor the food processor, nor the government can guarantee with absolute certainty that the food you eat will be free of pathogens. Remember the rules of food safety, and remember that you are the last link in the food safety chain.

# Q & A

**Q.** I keep hearing about foodborne diseases caused by contaminated meat and chicken. Should I become a vegetarian?

**A.** Many people are vegetarians for health reasons or because they do not believe it is right to eat meat. But fear of getting a foodborne disease is not a good reason to avoid meat, poultry, or fish. Properly cooked, they are safe and nutritious. The mainstays of the vegetarian diet, fruits and vegetables, can also carry disease-causing microbes. Your best bet is to develop good food safety habits.

**Q.** I ordered chicken in a restaurant, but when I cut it open, it was still pink inside. What should I have done?

**A.** You should have sent the chicken back to the kitchen, explaining that it was undercooked. The chef should be happy to correct the mistake.

**Q.** I am hungry for a midnight snack. That pizza on the table, left over from dinner, looks good. Is it safe to eat if I warm it up in the microwave?

**A.** No, it is not safe. Bacteria grow rapidly at room temperature, and many produce toxins that are heat-resistant. Even if microwaving the pizza does kill all the microbes (a risky assumption), their toxins could still make you sick.

**Q.** Is it a good idea to use antibacterial soaps when I am in the kitchen?

**A.** Not necessarily. A good soap and hot water is all that is needed to get your hands clean. In fact, some food safety experts worry that the widespread use of antibacterial soaps may result in the emergence of resistant strains of microbes.

**Q.** Why is it okay to eat steak that is pink inside, but not hamburgers?

**A.** All the microbes on a cut of meat, such as steak, are carried on the surface of the meat. These microbes are killed when the steak is cooked—assuming the chef does not use a sharp fork to turn the meat, which could drive surface microbes into the interior. But the organisms in ground meat, such as hamburger, are distributed throughout the meat, so the inside of the burger is no different, microbially speaking, from the outside.

**Q.** The top of a can of green beans in our cupboard is bulging. What should I do?

**A.** Do not open the can. The beans may be contaminated with *Clostridium botulinum*, which produces a gas that causes cans to bulge. The toxin it produces is so potent that even a tiny bit can make you very ill. Take the can to the grocery store so the store manager can contact the company that canned the beans.

**Q.** Do I need to wash produce labeled *organic* or *prewashed*?

**A.** Yes. All produce, including organically grown produce, can be contaminated with harmful organisms. "Prewashed" produce is not necessarily free of microbes and has in the past been responsible for foodborne disease.

**Q.** I have been vomiting, with nausea, diarrhea, and a fever, for the better part of a day. I cannot keep anything down. Should I call the doctor?

**A.** Yes, you should call your doctor. If you have not been able to keep fluids down for the better part of a day and especially if you feel dehydrated, you should seek medical attention.

**Q.** I had a *Salmonella* infection. My doctor said I might be infectious even after I feel better. How can I prevent spreading the infection to others?

**A.** Wash your hands. This is one of the most important things you and anyone else can do to avoid infecting others. Use warm, soapy water for at least twenty seconds after using the bathroom and before handling food.

**Q.** How long can I safely keep a package of lunch meat in the refrigerator?

**A.** Unopened packages keep well for two weeks; throw out opened packages after three to five days.

# Food Poisoning and Foodborne Diseases Timeline

1857—William Taylor, in Penrith, England, shows that milk can transmit typhoid fever.

1880—Germany begins the commercial pasteurization of milk; the United States follows suit in 1890.

1888—A. Gärtner isolates *Salmonella enteritidis* from meat that caused fifty-nine cases of foodborne disease.

1895—Emile van Ermengen shows that botulism is caused by a spore-forming bacteria, *Clostridium botulinum*.

1914—M. A. Barber shows that *Staphylococcus aureus* causes food poisoning; in 1930 Gail M. Dack proves that staph food poisoning is actually caused by a microbial toxin.

1929—France issues patent for the use of high-energy radiation in processing foods.

1938—Investigators traces outbreaks of *Campylobacter* infections to milk in Illinois.

1943—B. E. Proctor uses ionizing radiation to preserve hamburger meat.

1945—McClung shows that *Clostridium perfringens* can cause food poisoning.

1971—First documented outbreak of *Escherichia coli* foodborne gastroenteritis in the United States.

1976—Infant botulism first recognized in California.

1977—Martin Skirrow isolates *Campylobacter jejuni* from patients with diarrhea, and implicates chickens.

1978—First documented foodborne outbreak of gastroenteritis caused by the Norwalk virus, in Australia.

1981—First documented foodborne outbreak of listeriosis in the United States.

1982—First foodborne outbreaks of disease caused by *E. coli* O157:H7 in the United States.

1990—FDA approves the irradiation of poultry.

1997—FDA approves the irradiation of red meat.

# For More Information

You can learn more about foodborne diseases and food poisoning, and how to prevent them from happening to you, from your local County Extension Office. You will find them listed in the blue (government) pages of your local phone book.

**Center for Food Safety and Applied Nutrition (CFSAN)**
**Food and Drug Administration**
200 C Street SW
Washington, DC 20204

**Food Information & Seafood Hotline**
(800) FDA-4010
http://vm.cfsan.fda.gov/list.html
For detailed information about individual pathogens, visit the "Bad Bug Book" at http://vm.cfsan.fda.gov/~mow/intro.html

**Centers for Disease Control and Prevention (CDC)**
1600 Clifton Road NE
Atlanta, GA 30333
(404) 639-3311
http://www.cdc.gov

**Council for Agricultural Science and Technology (CAST)**
4420 West Lincoln Way
Ames, IA 50014-3447
(515) 292-2125
Fax: (515) 292-4512
http://www.cast-science.org/

**Food Safety and Inspection Service (FSIS)**
U.S. Department of Agriculture
FSIS Food Safety Education and Communications Staff
Room 1175, South Building
1400 Independence Avenue SW
Washington, DC 20250
Meat and Poultry Hotline: (800) 535-4555
(202) 720-7943
Fax: (202) 720-1843
http://www.fsis.usda.gov

**Safe Tables Our Priority (STOP)**
335 Court Street, Suite 100
Brooklyn, NY 11231
(718) 246-2739
Fax: (718) 624-4267
Hotline: (800) 350-STOP
http://www.stop-usa.org

**World Health Organization (WHO)**
Avenue Appia 20
1211 Geneva 27
Switzerland
http://www.who.ch/

# Chapter Notes

## Chapter 1. Foodborne Disease Today

1. Centers for Disease Control and Prevention, "Update: Multistate Outbreak of *Escherichia coli* O157:H7 Infections from Hamburgers—Western United States, 1992–1993," *Morbidity and Mortality Weekly Report*, vol. 42, no. 14, April 16, 1993.

2. Suzanne Kiner, interview with the author, March 6, 1998.

3. Ibid.

4. Nancy H. Bean, Joy S. Goulding, Christopher Lao, and Frederick J. Angulo, "Surveillance for Foodborne-Disease Outbreaks—United States, 1988–1992," *CDC Surveillance Summaries, Morbidity and Mortality Weekly Report*, vol. 45, no. SS-5, October 25, 1996, pp. 1–65.

5. World Health Organization, "Food Safety—a Worldwide Public Health Issue," *WHO-OMS*, 1998, <http://www.who.org/fsf/fctshtfs.htm> (October 21, 1998).

6. Council for Agricultural Science and Technology, *Foodborne Pathogens: Risks and Consequences*, Task Force Report No. 122, September 1994, p. 1.

7. Jean C. Buzby, Tanya Roberts, C.-T. Jordan Lin, and James M. MacDonald, *Bacterial Foodborne Disease: Medical Costs and Productivity Losses*, Food and Consumer Economics Division, Economic Research Service, U.S. Department of Agriculture, Agricultural Economic Report No. 741, August 1996.

## Chapter 2. The History of Foodborne Disease

1. E. M. Foster, "A Half Century of Food Microbiology," *Food Technology*, September 1989, pp. 208–215.

2. Jack Meadows, *The Great Scientists* (New York: Oxford University Press, 1987; reprinted 1992, 1994), p. 181.

3. Emile van Ermengem, *A New Anaerobic Bacillus and Its Relation to Botulism* (originally published as "Uber einen neuen anaëroben Bacillus und seine Beziehungen zum Botulismus," in *Zeitschrift für Hygiene und Infektionskrankheiten*, vol. 26, 1897, pp. 1–56), Sam Desch, translator, *Reviews of Infectious Diseases*, vol. 1, July–August 1979, pp. 701–719.

4. Bibek Ray, *Fundamental Food Microbiology* (Boca Raton, Fla.: CRC Press, 1996), pp. 278–279.

5. W. H. Stewart, "A Mandate for State Action," presented to the Association of State and Territorial Health Officers, Washington, D.C., December 4, 1967.

6. S. F. Altekruse, M. L. Cohen, and D. L. Swerdlow, "Emerging Foodborne Diseases," *Emerging Infectious Diseases*, vol. 3, no. 3, 1997, pp. 285–293.

7. Joan Stephenson, "Public Health Experts Take Aim at a Moving Target: Foodborne Infections," *Journal of the American Medical Association*, vol. 277, no. 2, 1997, pp. 97–98.

8. B. B. Chomel, E. E. DeBess, D. M. Mangiamele, et al., "Changing Trends in the Epidemiology of Human Brucellosis in California from 1973 to 1992: A Shift toward Foodborne Transmission," *Journal of Infectious Disease*, vol. 170, 1994, pp. 1216–1223.

9. D. Bell, "Forces That Have Helped Shape the U.S. Egg Industry: The Last 100 Years," *Poultry Tribune*, 1995, pp. 30–43.

10. Caroline A. Ryan, Mary K. Nickels, Nancy T. Hargrett-Bean et al., "Massive Outbreak of Antimicrobial-Resistant Salmonellosis Traced to Pasteurized Milk," *Journal of the American Medical Association*, vol. 258, no. 22, 1987, pp. 3269–3274.

11. Laurie Garrett, *The Coming Plague: Newly Emerging Diseases in a World Out of Balance* (New York: Farrar, Straus and Giroux, 1994), p. 427.

12. M. B. Skirrow, "Campylobacter Enteritis: A "New" Disease," *British Medical Journal*, vol. 2, no. 6078, July 2, 1977, pp. 9–11.

13. Ruth L. Berkelman, Ralph T. Bryan, Michael T. Osterholm et al., "Infectious Disease Surveillance: A Crumbling Foundation," *Science*, vol. 264, April 15, 1994, pp. 368–370.

## Chapter 3. How Our Bodies Fight Back

1. Michael Osterholm, interview with Terry Gross, *Fresh Air*, National Public Radio, May 5, 1998.

2. Irene V. Wesley, "*Helicobacter and Arcobacter*: Potential Human Foodborne Pathogens?" *Trends in Food Science & Technology*, vol. 8, September 1997, pp. 293–299.

## Chapter 4. A Gallery of Microbes

1. Charles Onufer, interview with the author, March 16, 1998.

2. S. F. Altekruse, M. L. Cohen, and D. L. Swerdlow, "Emerging Foodborne Diseases," *Emerging Infectious Diseases*, vol. 3, no. 3, 1997, pp. 285–293.

3. Consumers Union of U.S., Inc., "Chicken: What You Don't Know Can Hurt You," *Consumer Reports Online*, March 1998, <http://www.consumerreports.org/@RCXMqoYMuYnylhAA/Categories/FoodHealth/> (October 21, 1998).

4. U.S. Food and Drug Administration and Center for Food Safety & Applied Nutrition, *"Campylobacter jejuni,"* *Foodborne Pathogenic Microorganisms and Natural Toxins Handbook,* January 1992, <http://vm.cfsan.fda.gov/~mow/chap4.html> (October 21, 1998).

5. Altekruse et al., pp. 285–293.

6. Consumers Union of U. S., Inc.,

7. U.S. Food and Drug Administration and Center for Food Safety & Applied Nutrition, *"Salmonella* spp.," *Foodborne Pathogenic Microorganisms and Natural Toxins Handbook,* January 1992, <http://vm.cfsan.fda.gov/~mow/chap1.html> (October 21, 1998).

8. Altekruse et al., pp. 285–293.

9. Christopher Drew and Pam Belluck, "Deadly Bacteria a New Threat to Fruit and Produce in the U.S.," *The New York Times,* January 4, 1998, p. A1; Pam Belluck and Christopher Drew, "Tracing Bout of Illness to Small Lettuce Farm," *The New York Times,* January 5, 1998, p. A1.

10. U.S. Food and Drug Administration and Center for Food Safety & Applied Nutrition, *"Escherichia coli* O157:H7," *Foodborne Pathogenic Microorganisms and Natural Toxins Handbook,* January 1992, <http://vm.cfsan.fda.gov/~mow/chap15.html> (October 21, 1998).

11. Centers for Disease Control and Prevention: Division of Bacterial and Mycotic Diseases, National Center for Infectious Diseases, "Questions and Answers about *Vibrio vulnificus,"* April 1, 1997, <http://www.cdc.gov/ncidod/diseases/foodborn/vibriovu.htm> (October 21, 1998).

12. Centers for Disease Control and Prevention: Division of Bacterial and Mycotic Diseases, National Center for Infectious Diseases, "Preventing Foodborne Illness: Listeriosis," n.d., <http://www.cdc.gov/ncidod/publications/brochures/lister.htm> (October 21, 1998).

13. Ibid.

14. U.S. Food and Drug Administration and Center for Food Safety & Applied Nutrition, "Hepatitis A Virus," *Foodborne Pathogenic Microorganisms and Natural Toxins Handbook*, April 1991, <http://vm.cfsan.fda.gov/~mow/chap31.html> (May 1, 1998).

15. UK Ministry of Agriculture, Fisheries, and Food, "MAFF BSE Information: Incidence of BSE," 1998, <http://www.maff.gov.uk/animalh/bse/bse-statistics/level-3-incidence.html#general> (October 21, 1998).

## Chapter 5. Diagnosis and Treatment

1. Carrie McGraw, interview with the author, May 1998.

2. Terry McGraw, interview with the author, April 1998.

3. Caroline A. Ryan, Mary K. Nickels, Nancy T. Hargrett-Bean et al., "Massive Outbreak of Antimicrobial-Resistant Salmonellosis Traced to Pasteurized Milk," *Journal of the American Medical Association*, vol. 258, no. 22, 1987, pp. 3269–3274.

4. Thomas W. Hennessy et al., "A National Outbreak of *Salmonella enteritidis* Infections from Ice Cream," *New England Journal of Medicine*, vol. 334, 1996, pp. 1281–1286.

5. Kate Glynn, interview with the author, May 18, 1998.

6. Raymond Chung, interview with the author, May 28, 1998.

7. Ibid.

8. Ibid.

9. Ibid.

10. Glynn.

11. Ibid.

12. Ibid.

13. Ibid.

14. Ibid.

## Chapter 6. Prevention

1. Patricia Conlin, interview with the author, April 13, 1998.

2. Janet Raloff, "Tracking and Tackling Foodborne Germs," *Science News*, May 25, 1996, p. 326.

3. Janet Raloff, "Sponges and Sinks and Rags, Oh My! Where Microbes Lurk and How to Rout Them," *Science News*, September 14, 1996, p. 172.

4. C.-T. Jordan Lin, Roberta A. Morales, and Katherine Ralston, "Raw and Undercooked Eggs: A Danger of Salmonellosis," *Food Safety*, January–April 1997, pp. 27–32.

5. Suzanne Kiner, interview with the author, March 6, 1998.

6. M. Iwaki, "*E. coli* Can Exist Inside Radish Sprouts," presented at the International Conference on Emerging Infectious Diseases, March 8–11, 1998.

7. G. E. Bell, "Foodborne Pathogen Resists Washing," presented at the International Conference on Emerging Infectious Diseases, March 8–11, 1998.

8. Marion Burros, "Official Advice: Eat as I Say, Not as I Do," *The New York Times*, December 10, 1997, p. B1.

9. Ibid.

10. John de Louvois and Anita Rampling, "One Fifth of Samples of Unpasteurised Milk Are Contaminated with Bacteria," *British Medical Journal*, February 21, 1998, p. 625.

## Chapter 7. The High Cost to Society

1. Nancy Donley, interview with the author, May 4, 1998.

2. Council for Agricultural Science and Technology, *Foodborne Pathogens: Risks and Consequences*, Task Force Report No. 122, September 1994, p. 1.

3. T. G. Boyce, D. L. Swerdlow, and P. M. Griffin, "*Escherichia coli* O157:H7 and the Hemolytic-uremic Syndrome," *New England Journal of Medicine*, vol. 333, 1995, pp. 364–368.

4. Anne Schuchat, Bala Swaminathan, and Claire V. Broome, "Epidemiology of Human Listeriosis," *Clinical Microbiology Reviews*, vol. 4, no. 2, 1991, pp. 169–183.

5. Jean C. Buzby and Tanya Roberts, "Guillain-Barré Syndrome Increases Foodborne Disease Costs," *Food Review*, September–December 1997, pp. 36–42.

6. Ibid.

7. World Health Organization, "Food Safety—A Worldwide Public Health Issue," *WHO-OMS*, 1998, <http://www.who.org/fsf/fctshtfs.htm> (October 21, 1998).

8. Fritz K. Käferstein, "Food Safety: A Commonly Underestimated Public Health Issue—Introduction," *World Health Statistics Quarterly*, vol. 50, World Health Organization, Geneva, Switzerland, 1997, pp. 3–4.

9. Donley, interview.

## Chapter 8. New Directions in Food Safety

1. Sue Doneth, interview with the author, April 29, 1998.

2. Jeff Gerth and Tim Weiner, "Imports Swamp U.S. Food-Safety Efforts," *The New York Times*, September 29, 1997, p. A1.

3. William Jefferson Clinton, "Radio Address of the President to the Nation," January 25, 1997, <http://www.whitehouse.gov/WH/html/1997-01-25.html> (October 21, 1998).

4. B. E. Mahon et al., "An International Outbreak of *Salmonella* Infections Caused by Alfalfa Sprouts Grown from Contaminated Seed," *Journal of Infectious Disease*, vol. 175, 1997, pp. 876–882.

5. Joan Stephenson, "Public Health Experts Take Aim at a Moving Target: Foodborne Infections," *Journal of the American Medical Association*, vol. 277, no. 2, January 8, 1997, pp. 97–98.

6. Guodong Wang, Tong Zhao, and Michael P. Doyle, "Fate of Enterohemorrhagic *Escherichia coli* O157:H7 in Bovine Feces," *Applied Microbiology*, vol. 62, no. 7, 1996, p. 2567.

7. Robert Tauxe, "Does Organic Gardening Foster Foodborne Pathogens?—Reply," *Journal of the American Medical Association*, vol. 277, 1997, p. 1680.

8. Dean Cliver, interview with the author, April 30, 1998.

9. Gina Kolata, "F.D.A., Saying Process Is Safe, Approves Irradiating Red Meat," *The New York Times*, December 3, 1997, p. A1.

10. Michael T. Osterholm and Morris E. Potter, "Irradiation Pasteurization of Solid Foods: Taking Food Safety to the Next Level," *Emerging Infectious Diseases*, vol. 3, no. 4, Centers for Disease Control, 1997, pp. 575–577.

11. P. J. Skerrett, "Food Irradiation: Will It Keep the Doctor Away?" *Technology Review*, vol. 100, no. 8, 1997, p. 28.

12. Fred Breidt and Henry P. Fleming, "Using Lactic Acid Bacteria to Improve the Safety of Minimally Processed Fruits and Vegetables," *Food Technology*, vol. 51, no. 9, September 1997, pp. 44–49.

13. Dee M. Graham, "Use of Ozone for Food Processing," *Food Technology*, vol. 51, no. 6, June 1997, pp. 72–75.

14. Michael Doyle, interview with the author, May 8, 1998.

15. Carl Batt, interview with the author, April 1998.

16. Hans Blaschek, interview with the author, April 1998.

17. C. O. Tacket et al., "Immunogenicity in Humans of a Recombinant Bacterial Antigen Delivered in a Transgenic Potato," *Nature Medicine*, vol. 4, no. 5, May 1998, pp. 607–609.

18. N. Kiyatkin, A. B. Maksymowych, and L. L. Simpson, "Induction of an Immune Response by Oral Administration of Recombinant Botulinum Toxin," *Infection and Immunity*, vol. 65, no. 11, November 1997, pp. 4586–4591.

19. Laurie Garrett, *The Coming Plague: Newly Emerging Diseases in a World Out of Balance* (New York: Farrar, Straus and Giroux, 1994), p. 427.

20. Michael Osterholm, interview with Terry Gross, *Fresh Air*, National Public Radio, May 5, 1998.

# Glossary

**antibiotic resistance**—The ability developed by some microorganisms to survive the effects of antibiotics.

**antibiotics**—Substances that can kill or inhibit the growth of microorganisms; produced naturally by certain fungi, bacteria, and other microorganisms, or synthetically by drug chemists in the laboratory.

**bacteria**—Microscopic, one-celled organisms; unlike plant or animal cells, bacteria do not have a separate nucleus bounded by a membrane.

**botulism**—Food poisoning caused by a toxin produced by the bacterium *Clostridium botulinum*; the toxin attacks the nervous system and can cause muscle weakness, paralysis, and death.

**bovine spongiform encephalopathy (BSE)**—A rare, fatal disease affecting the brain and central nervous system of cattle; popularly known as mad cow disease, BSE is thought to be caused by a type of rogue protein known as a prion, transmitted through contaminated animal feed.

**campylobacteriosis**—A foodborne infection caused by the *Campylobacter jejuni* bacterium.

**carrier**—A person or animal that harbors and spreads an organism that causes disease; the carrier is generally either immune to the effects of the organism or has recovered from being infected.

cross-contamination—The transfer of pathogens from one food, surface, or person to another.

danger zone—The range of temperatures at which most bacteria multiply rapidly, between 40°F and 140°F.

DNA—Deoxyribonucleic acid, the molecule that carries genetic information for all forms of life.

electrolyte—A nonmetallic substance that when dissolved in water can conduct an electrical current; some electrolytes, including potassium and sodium, are essential to our bodies' cells.

epidemic—The rapid spread of a contagious disease, affecting a large number of individuals in a population or region at the same time.

feces—Solid waste products excreted from the bowels.

foodborne infection—Illness caused by eating food contaminated with certain kinds of microorganisms, which can continue to live and grow inside the body.

foodborne intoxication—Illness caused by eating foods contaminated with a toxin produced by bacteria or molds.

gastroenteritis—Inflammation of the lining of the stomach and intestines, often caused by a foodborne infection.

gastrointestinal tract—The stomach and intestines.

Guillain-Barré syndrome (GBS)—A disease that affects the nerves of the body and can lead to paralysis; as many as 40 percent of GBS cases in this country may be triggered by a *Campylobacter* infection.

hemolytic uremic syndrome—A complication of *E. coli* O157:H7 infections, especially in young children, in which the red blood cells are destroyed and the kidneys fail.

**hepatitis**—Inflammation of the liver.

**irradiation**—A process of exposing foods to high-energy, invisible waves (radiation) to kill harmful microorganisms.

**isolate**—An individual or strain obtained from a natural population; also the action of separating one group or individual from others.

**jaundice**—A yellowish tinge to the skin and tissues caused by bile pigments; a common symptom of liver disease.

**listeriosis**—An infection with *Listeria monocytogenes*, a bacterium that can be found in vegetables, milk, cheese, meat, and seafood.

**microorganism**—A general term for bacteria, viruses, or parasites that can be seen only with a microscope.

**normal flora**—Harmless bacteria that normally reside in the intestines.

**outbreak**—An increase in the number of cases of disease in a group of people or region.

**parasite**—Any organism that lives on or in another organism on which it feeds; strictly speaking, bacteria, viruses, and fungi could be called parasites, but in practice the term is usually reserved for some kinds of protozoa and worms.

**pasteurization**—The process used to destroy foodborne pathogens; when used alone, usually refers to a heating process.

**pathogen**—A disease-causing microorganism.

**protozoan**—A single-celled, usually microscopic organism, larger and more complex in structure than bacteria; many are harmless, but some are parasitic and can cause disease.

**salmonellosis**—An infection with one of the *Salmonella* bacteria.

**spore**—A dormant stage of bacteria, covered with a hard, protective coat.

**toxin**—A poisonous molecule, usually produced by a microorganism.

**"trots"**—A humorous way of referring to diarrhea.

**vaccine**—A pathogen made harmless by either killing or weakening it, and given to induce immunity to the pathogen; a vaccine may also be just part of the microbe or a microbial product.

**virus**—A small bundle of genes, protected by a protein coat; viruses can reproduce only by infecting a host cell and using its genetic machinery.

# Further Reading

## Books

Council for Agricultural Science and Technology. *Foodborne Pathogens: Risks and Consequences.* Task Force Report, December 1994.

Dixon, Bernard. *Power Unseen: How Microbes Rule the World.* Oxford, England: W. H. Freeman, 1996.

Fox, Nichols. *Spoiled: The Dangerous Truth About a Food Chain Gone Haywire.* New York: BasicBooks, 1997.

Hui, Y. H., J. Richard Gorham, K. D. Murrell, and Dean O. Cliver, eds. *Foodborne Disease Handbook.* New York: Marcel Dekker, 1994 (3 volumes).

Kalbacken, Joan. *Food Safety.* Danbury, Conn.: Children's Press, 1998.

Leonard, Barry, ed. *Food Safety from Farm to Table: A National Food-Safety Initiative.* Upland, Pa.: Diane Publishing Co., 1998.

## Articles

Belluck, Pam, and Christopher Drew. "Tracing a Bout of Illness to Small Lettuce Farm." *The New York Times,* January 5, 1998, p. A1.

Drew, Christopher, and Pam Belluck, "Deadly Bacteria a New Threat to Fruit and Produce in U.S." *The New York Times,* January 4, 1998, p. A1.

St. George, Donna. "A Harvest of Risk and Burden for Oystermen." *The New York Times,* February 17, 1998, p. A1.

———. "In Street Vendors' Smorgasbord, Threat of Sickness Lurks." *The New York Times*, May 17, 1998, p. A1.

Wilkinson, Sophie L. "Eating Safely in a Dirty World." *Chemical and Engineering News*, November 19, 1997, pp. 24–33.

## Video

United States Department of Agriculture. *The Danger Zone: A Food Safety Program for Teens.*

## Internet Addresses

### Food Safety Retrieval System

North Carolina Cooperative Extension Service. "Food Safety Information Retrieval System." October 21, 1998 <http://www.ces.ncsu.edu/depts/foodsci/agentinfo> (January 8, 1999).

### National Food Safety Database

The National Food Safety Database Project. "The National Food Safety Database." n.d. <http://www.foodsafety.org> (January 8, 1999).

# Index

Skirrow, Martin, 28
Smith, Patty, 66–67
Snow, John, 27
staph poisoning, 21–22, 47
*Staphylococcus aureus*, 21, 22, 32,
    35, 47, 60, 81, 95
Stewart, William H., 23
symptoms, 9, 12, 34, 38, 40,
    41–42, 43, 44, 46, 47, 49, 50,
    51, 52, 56, 57

**T**
Tauxe, Robert V., 91
Taylor, William, 18
*Toxoplasma gondii*, 81, 92
transmission, 30–32, 44, 50,
    51–52
treatment, 12, 57, 60
tuberculosis, 23
typhoid fever, 18–19, 23, 30, 34,
    40
Typhoid Mary, 30

**U**
United States Department of
    Agriculture (USDA), 13, 68,
    81, 90, 94–95

**V**
vaccines, 15, 96, 100
Van Ermengem, Emile, 21
Van Leeuwenhoek, Antonie, 17
*Vibrio*, 43–44, 46
    *cholerae*, 27, 35, 44
    *parahaemolyticus*, 44
    *vulnificus*, 44, 46
virus, 11, 14, 23, 51–52
vomit, 11, 22, 32, 35, 41, 44, 47,
    50, 51, 56

**W**
World Health Organization
    (WHO), 13,

**Y**
*Yersinia*, 59

128